CHAV!

A User's Guide to Britain's New Ruling Class

CHAV!

A User's Guide to Britain's New Ruling Class

By Mia Wallace and Clint Spanner

BANTAM BOOKS
LONDON • NEW YORK • TORONTO • SYDNEY • AUCKLAND

CHAV!
A BANTAM BOOK: 0 553 81713 2

First publication in Great Britain

PRINTING HISTORY
Bantam edition published 2004

7 9 10 8 6

Cover and inside illustrations by Jerry Paris
Additional inside illustrations by John Taylor

Set in Bookman Old Style

Bantam Books are published by Transworld Publishers,
61–63 Uxbridge Road, London W5 5SA,
a division of The Random House Group Ltd,
in Australia by Random House Australia (Pty) Ltd,
20 Alfred Street, Milsons Point, Sydney, NSW 2061, Australia,
in New Zealand by Random House New Zealand Ltd,
18 Poland Road, Glenfield, Auckland 10, New Zealand
and in South Africa by Random House (Pty) Ltd,
Endulini, 5a Jubilee Road, Parktown 2193, South Africa.

Printed and bound in Great Britain by
Mackays of Chatham plc, Chatham, Kent.

Papers used by Transworld Publishers are natural, recyclable products made from
wood grown in sustainable forests. The manufacturing processes conform to the
environmental regulations of the country of origin.

www.booksattransworld.co.uk

DEDICATION

This book is dedicated to our mums and dads, brothers and sisters, grandmas and grandpas, aunties and uncles, nieces and nephews and all the friends who have helped us along the way – and NOT to all those who haven't helped, and have, in fact, actively hindered us. You know who you are!

Hats off to crime
Please remove all hats
and hoods before entering
this establishment

ACKNOWLEDGEMENTS

Mia: Thank you to Jane Gunn and Jos Thomas for helping me to get what was in my head onto the page – and making it readable!

Clint: Thanks to Richard Hodd – without you the website and book would have never happened!

And finally and most importantly, thanks both of us to Brilliant Brenda, Slick Simon, Andy and Nick, this book's midwives, and to the design team: Claire, Hugh, Lord Philip, Jerry and John. Finally, thanks to Viv – for being the reason behind most things.

CONTENTS

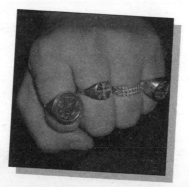

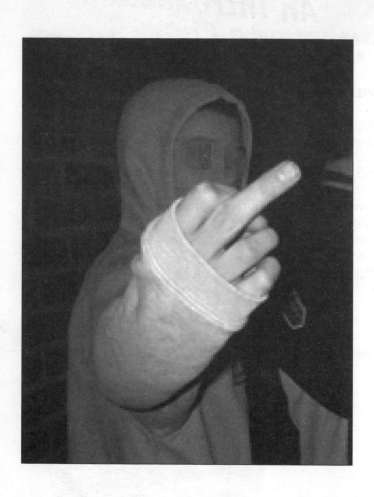

An Introduction to Chavs

WHAT IS A CHAV?

Well, you might not be able to describe them, but you know who they are and you know what they look like. You've seen the baseball caps, the Mr T. jewellery, trackie bottoms and trainers.

But Chav is so much more than this! It's an attitude, a way of life, a tribal thing, and those in it (or innit) have chosen to be there. Now, in this invaluable guide, you can check out the culture, the lifestyle, the language, the loves, likes and dislikes of this unique phenomenon – a phenomenon that began in Chatham and which is sweeping Britain – and a shopping centre near you every Saturday afternoon!

Welcome to the wonderful world of *CHAV!*

CHAV SPOTTING

The Essential Guide to Chav Spotting

A game the whole family can play! Spotting a chav in the wild is easy. Often moving around in packs like a strange nomadic tribe, the rigid dress code will enable you to spot a chav yards away. Cutting-edge, fake-designer fashion, branded sportswear and accessories to die for, fabulously extravagant 9-carat-gold 'bling' (jewellery), it's all here in this fun-for-all-the-family, point-scoring game! Let's start with...

Baseball Caps... You can almost disregard those worn at a jaunty angle – and even the ones worn back to front. Real chavs like to use their  caps (and hoods) to enhance the sense of mystery and danger they hope you will feel when you're around them, and, of course, to avoid being clocked by CCTV cameras! To score maximum points, you have to spot the right kind of chav cap! A plain-coloured cap will get you 5 points...one sporting a fake designer logo will get you 10, but if you sport the 'genuine' fake Burberry cap – the ultimate chavster accessory available on a market stall near you – give yourself a massive 15 points.

Branded Shirts and Jackets...

Forget Savile Row tailoring, what your average chav-about-town likes to be seen in is branded sportswear – and the bigger the brand name the better! Look out for what was this summer's classic, the pink Nickelson polo shirt and this winter's classic, the sky-blue McKenzie hoody;

✱

What your average chav-about-town likes to be seen in is branded sportswear.

✱

award yourself 10 points for each. But if you manage to spot some half-arsed, washed-out piece of tat with most of the lettering peeling off, and which you know half the family has worn throughout the year, give

yourself a 2-point bonus. As for the FCUK zip-up hoody, chavs specialize in cheap fakes and they don't come much cheaper or more fake than this one because the brand don't even make a version of it. Add 10 bonus points for this beauty.

Tracksuits and Shell Suits... Give

yourself 10 points for every 'designer' set, and a further 5 bonus points every time you spot a mismatched trackie top and bottom. If you're lucky enough to find a chav teaming a pair of trackie bottoms with something entirely different – say, a velvet shirt or a highly patterned jumper, give yourself a big 5-point bonus. The real winner in this category is the classic white Shell Suit. But remember, if it's white you've just gotta wear shades and plenty of bling. You earn a massive 20 points if you spot a chav wearing the whole ensemble!

Trainers... Most chavs don't own a pair of

shoes – all they have are white trainers. And like all chav attire, a prominent, chav-respected brand name is a must! (Unbranded trainers from the market will only get you, as they say in the Eurovision Song Contest, Nil Points.) Chav trainers must be 'prison-white' clean to make it look like they've just been bought. (Deduct 2 points for any scuffmarks or stains.) It's a tough one, but for a massive 15 bonus points, try to spot a pair of sparkling white Reebok Classics – trainer nirvana to most chavs – which are usually only worn for weddings or funerals, so are much harder to spot.

'Nil points'

Handbags... The 'Louis' (Vuitton) handbag will get you 10 points – but add 2 points for obviously plastic handles and broken zips – or if you spot one in 'Paaandland' or the Dole Office. The classic Burberry handbag will also get you 10, but add 5 points if the fake print is so bad it looks wobbly, or as if the chav has wandered into McChav territory with a strange new tartan.

Jewellery – Bling! Bling! Bling!... Gold Clown Pendants – fabulously big, bold and brassy; give yourself 15 points for every one you spot, but look out for other variants, such as a rag doll, teddy bear, horse, gypsy caravan, gun and a clown with a pushchair. Chavs will wear their pendants outside any garment and on full display, so you won't have to work too hard to spot these. **Thick Gold Chains** – in the style of Mr T. – will get you 10 points, but only if they're at least 5mm thick. (Size matters to chavs!) Add another 5 points if they look chunky enough to double up as a dog lead. **Sovereign Rings** – once the hallmark of the cockney villain, scrap merchant and Sir

Jimmy Saville, the 'sov' has now been embraced by the chav, especially the faux 'sov' – **the Medallion Ring**. This classy piece of hand furniture is supposed to make the wearer look rich, but also comes in handy for giving the missus a backhander! Score 15 points for every sovereign you spot, and add 5 if they're slightly bent or have obviously been

used in a fight. **BIG Hoop Gold Earrings:** nothing says 'filthy chavette' quite like a nice thick pair of big hoop gold earrings! Score 15 points for every massive 9-carat-gold

*

Look out for other variants, such as a rag doll, teddy bear, horse, gypsy caravan, gun and a clown with a pushchair.

*

hollow hoop. You can add 5 more if they're big enough for a budgie to swing on, 10 if a police dog could jump through them, and 15 if they actually rest on the chavette's shoulders. Those sporting a set of diamondesque-encrusted balls on each earring – the absolute ultimate

bling-bling hoop – will get you a massive 10-point bonus. **The huge Gold Cross** is, of course, an essential chav accessory – 15 points – but add an extra 5 points if any of the cubic zircs have fallen out, and a further 2 if the chain looks paper thin and dented. The fake **Tiffany Heart Pendant**, another must for all chavettes, will earn the chav spotter a nice little 10-pointer. However, for a terrific 5 bonus points, try to spot one that has turned the wearer's neck green. The final bit of bling has to be **the Ankle Chain**, possibly the chavette's trashiest 9-carat accessory. And because a chav needs to find as many places to hang her bling, in the summer the ankle chains come out in force. Again, you can score higher points depending on the thickness of the chain and can also get an extra point for each tacky charm you spot. (Not that a chavette would know, but in biblical times these were a sign that the wearer was a prostitute. However, if she did know this it would probably only make her happy that someone, some-time, got paid for what she generally gives away for free.) If the chain says something like 'bitch' or 'tart', you can add 5 more points – and you can double that if it's the same phrase as that written on the arse of her

AWARD YOURSELF 10 POINTS FOR SPOTTING:

Pink Nickelson polo shirt or sky-blue McKenzie hoody

The 'Louis' (Vuitton) or classic Burberry handbag

Thick pair of big hoopy gold earrings

15 POINTS FOR:

Fake Burberry baseball cap

A pair of sparkling white Reebok Classics

20 POINTS FOR:

White Shell Suit with shades and plenty of bling

Pierced 'tribal' pattern shaved eyebrow

Faux-gem-encrusted huge gold cross

30 POINTS FOR:

Chav baby with pierced ears/ earrings that are bigger than the baby

ADD 10 BONUS POINTS FOR:

the FCUK zip-up hoody

jeans. Points will be removed, however, if the chain in any way impairs the view of her ankle tattoo.

Piercings... Let's begin with the chavlings...For a whopping 15 points, look out for a chav baby with pierced ears. And if you can spot one with earrings that are bigger than the baby, or one with multiple earrings in each ear, give yourself another 15 bonus points. For the adults, **the Belly Button Piercing** is an absolute must-have. Score 20 points for each one you spot and another 10 for any that are obviously infected! **Tongue Piercings** will get you a further 30 points, but deduct 5 points if this has not made the chav lisp and froth at the mouth when they talk. **Eyebrow Piercings**, so popular with the younger set, will get you 15 points but add 5 more if the eyebrow has a 'tribal-rude-boy' pattern shaved into it.

Tattoos... Sailors' Tattoos are very popular, so should be quite easy to spot. Award yourself 10 points for every one you see, and 5 more for misspellings. Not quite so common are the **Scroll Tattoos**, which list the names of the chavlings in the dynasty, but you can earn 5 points for each name and a further 5 for abbreviations (Chaz, Daz, Gaz, Baz...). At heart, chavs are romantics, and when they change partners, they try to block out their ex-partner's name – but not always successfully. Score 10 points if you spot an obvious cover-up – a black bar is the option they usually go for. The really scummy Lothario's arm will resemble a bar code.

Hair and Hair Styles... For the boys, cropped or long, gelled or waxed, it doesn't really matter because most chavs wear their baseball caps all day, every day – and most of the night too. (Score 10 if you spot one without his cap!) As for girlies, 10 points can be awarded for spotting any of the following: greasy roots, black roots,

Score 15 points for Burberry-style check in anything.

bad bleach job or perm, gluey- or matted-looking texture which attracts flies (a clear indication of the overuse of cheap hair products). The classic look will always be the scraped back hair in a scrunchie – commonly known as the **'Romford Facelift'** – and this will win you 20 points. Add an extra 5 if it's a Burberry scrunchie.

Miscellaneous... Score 15 points for Burberry-style check in anything – umbrellas, shoes, tights, scarves – but if the item is anything particularly unusual, such as wellingtons or an eye-patch, then give yourself another 10 points. Spotting a really bad **Fake Tan** will get 5 Points but add 2 more for the day-glo orange, streakier versions. (Check the harder-to-reach areas, such as the back of the legs.) Spotting badly applied **Make-up** – caked on and either much too orange or much too pale – will get you 10 points, but you can carn bonus points here if the chavette in question has attempted to cover her zits with dollops of gluey foundation. And talking of unsightly blemishes, score 5 points for every **Love Bite** you spot. (This is where you can double your score because chavs love nothing more than displaying their bruised bits!) **Smoking** will also help you notch up your score. Score 10 for every chain-smoker you spot, and a further 10 if you catch them lighting their next fag from the butt of their first.

The Chav Snog is a thing to behold – and behold it you will in every shopping centre, pub or park – in fact *anywhere* public! Score 10 for snogging sessions lasting more than 10 minutes (easy-peasy) and a further 10 for any fondling that goes on whilst the snog is in progress!

This short guide will, hopefully, give you hours of entertainment – and, at the same time, introduce you to the rich, rude world of the chav. Remember to record your scores for future use and write down anything unusual you see that's not on

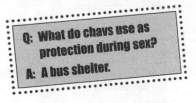

Q: What do chavs use as protection during sex?
A: A bus shelter.

the list. Just one word of warning before you begin... although this is a seemingly harmless and fun game, **Chav Spotting** can be quite addictive and you could even find yourself gawping at passers-by for hours on end in what might be a very chav-like way. Beware!

CHAVSPEAK

There are many different chav dialects around the country, but by far the most popular is 'Fuckwitspeak'. This dialect is spoken by chavs in East Anglia, London and the Home Counties but is spreading fast to the South West and the Midlands. Broadly speaking, it is a combination of Jamaican Yardie and Estuarine English – a sort of hybrid cockney.

Parlez vous 'Fuckwitspeak'?

Before you try a few basic words to get you started, here are some helpful hints in case you want to converse with a chav...

- **Try to make your voice sound as nasal as possible.**

- **Try not to open your mouth too much. (Chavs are like dogs: if you expose your teeth, they see it as threat!)**

- **Try to make your words sound as whiney as possible. This is essential, as you will find that chavs will often replace a consonant with a slow, monotone whiney sound!**

Right, let's get started with some basic words...

Abaaaht – About

Aint(cha) – Aren't(you)

Awight – All right

Burgaa – Hamburger

Daahn – Down

Giss – Give

Gaahna – Going to

Git – Get

Laytaah – Later

Mingin' – Something nasty

Muvaaa – Mother

Moby – Mobile telephone

Shaaarup – Shut up

Naaah – No and Now

Taahn – Town

Tawkin – Talking

Yeah – Yes

Yerr – Your

So now let's put a few choice sentences together...

Lushinnit?
(Lovely, isn't it?)

Aaah ya gaahn daahn taahn laytaah?
(Will you be taking a trip into the town centre later?)

I'm aaahta cred-it.
(I have no credit left on my pay-as-you-go mobile
telephone.)

Got me trackies daahn primarkinnit. Well nice innit?
(I purchased my fetching tracksuit bottoms from Primark.
They're lovely, aren't they?)

Git outta 'ere.
(Go away, please.)

*Faaackin' shaaarup, Chesney! Ya muvaaas
tawkin' on 'er moby.*
(Would you please be quiet,
Chesney! Your mother is
trying to conduct a
conversation on her mobile
telephone.)

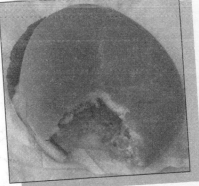

*You 'ad ya faaackin' burgaa,
naaah shaaarup!*
(You have had your
hamburger, now would you
please be quiet.)

Faakin' 'ell Chesney, yerr gunnaa faaackin' break vat chair doin' 'at!
(Chesney, would you please refrain from climbing on the furniture; you are liable to break that chair.)

Do vat again, Chesney, and I'll bleedin' beltchyerr one!
(Please don't do that again, Chesney, or I will be forced to administer some form of corporal punishment.)

Giss a faaag, mate?
(Excuse me, but can you let me have one of your cigarettes, please?)

I'll 'av a chazz burgaa.
(I think I'll have a cheese burger.)

> *Oi! Ge' us 3 Bacaaardibreezas, moosh.*

Paaand mate.
(That will be one pound, my good friend.)

Yerr wan' aany draw?
(Would you like to purchase some cannabis resin?)

Do yerr know where I caaan score raaaand 'ere, moosh?
(Would you happen to know where I can purchase some drugs?)

Gaaahna MaccyD's.
(I am going to the McDonald's restaurant.)

Oi! Ge' us 4 Bacaaardibreezas, moosh.
(Could you please break the law and purchase four Bacardi Breezers for me, as I am too young to buy alcohol.)

Oi! Couldyerr ge'us twenny Mayfair an' a scrachie.
(Could you please break the law and purchase twenty
Mayfair cigarettes and a lottery scratch card for me as I
am not yet sixteen years old?)

Awight, Stavros? I'll 'av a large donner.
(Hello, Greek Cypriot proprietor, I will have a large
donner kebab, please.)

*Yerr got any burgaa scauce for me chips? Nah? Just gis
the blaaahdy red sauce then! Sorted!*
(Do you have any of your lurid orange condiment that is
actually meant for beefburgers? No? Oh
well, in that case, please pass me
the tomato ketchup!)

Call vat a large chips? Yerr 'aving a faaackin' laarf aintcha?
(Are you jesting? I think this portion of chips is slightly smaller than it should be.)

> *Call vat a **large** chips? Yerr 'aving a faaackin' laarf, aintcha?*

I wanna go on vat. Giss 10ps for the machine, mate. I aint got none.
(I would like to have a flutter on your entertaining fruit machine. May I please have some 10p coins as I've run out of change?)

You should by now be getting an 'ear' for Chavspeak. However, during an argument, when situations get a little heated, Chavspeak can become almost indecipherable. In these circumstances, it is important to remember that chavs will say whatever it is they need to say in one long stream of vocalization. They will not pause for breath or stop to think about exactly what it is they are trying to say. As there is *nothing* a chav likes better than a row, in all the excitement they may actually forget to form coherent sentences and what comes out may just be a kind of screeching – or white noise! Here are a few examples of the sort of thing you may hear:

Wha'chooyoulookinatmoosh?
(Excuse me, but can I help you?)

Mindyerrownblaaahdybusiness!
(Sorry, but I really don't think this has anything to do with you.)

Yerrlookinferraslap?
(Are you trying to test my patience?)

Well, there you have it, a quick but handy guide to essential ChavSpeak. There's just one final tip for you: if you ever find yourself in a situation where you are forced to converse with a chav, just mumble incoherently but make sure at the same time that you drop into the conversation a few choice chav words (see above) and the names of famous designers or brand names. This will make the chav feel safe and secure while they try to decipher what you've said – and while you plan your get-away. And if all else fails and things get a little scary, just *'blaaahdy 'it 'em an' then run like 'ell!* Good luck!

CHAV CULTURE

Name Your Chav Baby

For all you mums and dads to be out there, here's the result of a recent chav poll to find the top twenty chavster names...

GIRLS

Chardonnay

1 Bethany
Origin: Old Ned / Corrie Kid
Meaning: Maker of bitchy comments
Also: Bethannie, Beffany, Beff

2 Chantelle
Origin: Old Chatham / Medway
Meaning: Wearer of bling and caked in make-up
Also: Chantel, Chanteal, 'Elle, Shantelle, Shant

3 Brandi
Origin: MTV / Off-licence
Meaning: She of the slurred speech and vague memory
Also: Chardonnay, Babycham, Brand, Logo

4 Chardonnay
Origin: Supermarket Shelf / *Footballers' Wives*
Meaning: Guzzler of BOGOF wines
Also: Brandi, Shar, Champagne, Lambrini,

Brandi

5 Bianca

Origin: *Eastenders* / Rock-star Wife
Meaning: She who staggers on white stilettos
Also: Beyanca, Beeanca, Biancca, Be-Anca, Bi, Be,
'Anca, Martini

6 Britney

Origin: Possibly French, more probably MTV / Trailer
Trash
Meaning: Shoplifts well (NB: Also good name for one half
of twins; see Whitney)
Also: Britnnay, Britnee, Britneay, Brit, Madonna

7 Shakira

Origin: MTV / Bad-Boy's Bitch
Meaning: Bringer of Pot Noodle
Also: Shakirraa, Shackierier, Alliah, Jamilla, Atomic-
Kitten

8 Tiffany

Origin: *Eastenders* / Hairdresser
Meaning: Keeper of small yappy dogs called Princess
Also: Tifany, Tiffney, Tiffphanny, Tiff, Jewel

9 Tracy

Origin: Unknown Chav Classic
Meaning: Unnaturally blond and dim
Also: Tracey, Trace, Sharron

10 Morgan
Origin: Semi-designer Shop
Meaning: She who dances with poles
Also: Morgann, Morganne, Miss Selfridge

11 Mercedes
Origin: TV Advertisement / Car Dealership
Meaning: She who likes to ride in the backseat of cars
Also: Porsche, Portia, Ferrari, Escort, Cortina

12 Whitney
Origin: Ancient MTV
Meaning: Decorated in Burberry (NB: Also good twin name; see Britney)
Also: Whitneay, Whitnee, Whit-Nee, Madonna, Cher

13 Sharron
Origin: *Eastenders* / Old Trailer Park / Chav Classic
Meaning: Bingo screecher / Market trader's delight
Also: Sharon, Sharrone, Shar, Shazza, Tracy

14 Jasmine
Origin: Flower of Chatham / Disney Princess
Meaning: Aroma of 'Paaandland' and ugly sulker
Also: Jazzmine, Jazmin, Jazz, Cinderella, Cindy, Ariel, Snow White

15 Crystal
Origin: Elizabeth Duke / Dynasty
Meaning: She who delights in bling
Also: Krystal, Krystalle, Christalle, Christie, Alexis,
Saphirre, 9ct, Jade

16 Courtney
Origin: Eastenders / MTV
Meaning: Pusher of double buggy
Also: Courtnay, Courtnee, Cortina, Cort

17 Kayleigh
Origin: 1980s Pop Tune
Meaning: Borrower of fags
Also: Kaylee, Kay-Leigh,
K-Li, Leigh, Rosanna, Roxanne, Rio

Kayleigh

18 Ashleigh
Origin: Ancient Rochester
Meaning: Scrunchied up, and up the duff
Also: Ashlee, Ashhleaigh, Ash-Lee, Ash, Lee

19 Hailey-Jayne
Origin: Ugly Corrie Sex-change Star / Old Mancunian
Meaning: Looks like a dog, howls like a wolf
Also: Hail-Lee, Haillee, Hail, Lee

20 Christina
Origin: Ancient Scouse / MTV
Meaning: She who lies to debt collectors
Also: Kristina, Christinnaa, Crista, Tina, Teen, Britney,
Pink

BOYS

1 Jordan
Origin: Basketball Icon /
Popular Make of Trainer
Meaning: Spitter of phlegm
Also: Jordann, Jord,
Jordy, Puma, Reebok-Classic

2 Brooklyn
Origin: Beckham Offspring
Meaning: 'Gangsta' wannabe
Also: Brookelin, Romeo, Manhattan, The Bronx
(*Not* to be confused with Queens!)

3 Brandon
Origin: Old Romford
Meaning: Seeker of benefits/Recipient of evil looks from
pensioners
Also: Brandonn, Brand, Logo

4 Alfie
Origin: *Eastenders* (NB: Not from the Michael Caine film
but there *will* be a resurgence after the forthcoming
Jude Law remake)
Meaning: He who buys stolen rubbish from pub
Also: Alfy, Alfee, Dirty Den, Mini-Den

5 Jason
Origin: Ancient Chav / Classic Chatham
Meaning: Wearer of baseball cap
Also: Jaason, Jasonn, Jase, J-son

6 Damian
Origin: Film about Antichrist
Meaning: He of much slapped legs / Terror of Tesco's
Also: Damien, Damiean, Damo, Satan, Beelzebub

Damian

7 Harrison
Origin: Action Hero / Beatle
Meaning: He of the gormless expression
Also: Harris, 'Arrison, 'Arris, Indiana, Lennon, Ringo

8 Jake
Origin: Unknown, but often attributed to Rolf Harris
Meaning: Teacher's burden
Also: J-Ake, Jakey, Jacksey

9 Kyle
Origin: Celtic / South Park
Meaning: Teeth of orthodontic nightmares
Also: Kail, Kialle, Stan, Kenny, Cartman

10 Jay
Origin: Jail Bird / Old Cardiff Park
Meaning: He who drives up and down
seafront in crap car
Also: Jaye, Jayee, Jay-Jay, JJ,
K, L or any letter of the alphabet

11 Billy-Bob-Jack
Origin: Mad Movie Star
Meaning: Sinister nutter covered in tattoos
Also: Jimmy-Joe, Billy-Jack (or any double- or triple-
barrelled name that sounds dumb)

12 Lee
Origin: Old Essex / Old East London (as in Valley)
Meaning: Father of many
Also: Leigh, Leeee, Le, Li, Lee-Lee, Lee-Li

13 Keanu
Origin: *The Matrix* / *The Royle Family*
Meaning: He who runs like a loon
Also: Keyanoo, Keyanu, Keeahnew, Kanoo, Morphius

Keanu

14 Wayne
Origin: Western hero / Harry Enfield
Meaning: Slack of jaw and covered in dribble
Also: Dwayne, Wayyne, Wain, Kevin, Perry

15 Kevin
Origin: Chav Classic / Harry Enfield
Meaning: Keeper of pitbulls
Also: Keevin, Kelvin, Kev, Kevster, Wayne, Perry

16 Elvis
Origin: Graceland / Memphis
Meaning: King of burger eaters
Also: 'Lvis, The King, Presley, Presser

17 Storm
Origin: *X-Men* / Exotic / Weather Warning
Meaning: He who takes on all-comers weekly in pub /
Farts in public
Also: Storme, Stormm, Wolverine, Hurricane, Tempest

18 Axel
Origin: Eddie Murphy Film / 1980s Rocker
Meaning: Modifer of cars
Also: Axell, Grease, Rocky, Rambo, Stallone, Slash, Bon-Jovi

19 Tyson
Origin: Boxer / Convicted Criminal
Meaning: He who pretends to be rock hard but is actually scared of loud girlfriend
Also: Tysonn, Ty, Bruno, Hulk, The Rock

20 Darren
Origin: Dagenham Market
Meaning: He who nicks wing mirrors off cars / Lets off bangers and rockets
Also: Dar-Ren, Daz, Dazed

The Chavster's Guide to Education

Education, Education, Education…or so it goes. Well, for most chavs education is a place named school that they sporadically attend between the age of five and being kicked out. The only reason a chav attends school even as much as twice a week is because they're bored with hanging around the shopping centres and dodging the police. Or because Mum has said that if she's up in court because of non-attendance one more time she will 'do 'em in' or simply to piss off any other kids at school who might want to learn something.

The Early Years… As a legal requirement, schooling must start at the age of five but for the chav this could be as much as a year earlier. Not because Mummy and Daddy have paid for early tutoring in an attempt to stretch their offspring's eager little mind, but because, where possible, they will lie about their sprog's age in order to get him off their hands a bit earlier.

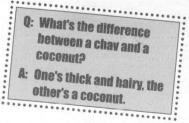

Q: What's the difference between a chav and a coconut?

A: One's thick and hairy, the other's a coconut.

In this new environment, the young chavling will encounter educational toys for the first time – books and writing instruments – and they will do what they are genetically programmed to do: destroy them. There is no

In the new school environment, the young chavling will encounter educational toys for the first time.

implement that cannot double up as a instrument of torture or vandalism, and any damage their older siblings can do with a compass, the chavling can do with some Unifix and a stickle brick. It's all a matter of application.

Chavs' Free Milk... In years gone by another good reason to send a child into school was the free milk. This was an entire half bottle of milk for the chavling and, such was his excitement, it was usually enough to send the little dear into shock or a fit of lactose-induced hysteria, which would kick-start the kid's bad behaviour for the rest of the morning. Luckily for the teachers, this freebie was abandoned some time ago. Without this fuel, the teachers could breathe a sigh of relief as the chavlings didn't have the energy to cause too much havoc until after their free meal...

Ah, the **Free Meal...** Knowing that the chavling would get at least one meal each day allows chav parents to spend the child benefit on vodka and fags guilt-free. Until the chavling is old enough to skank some cash for chips during the day, this meal is imperative and there's many a chav parent that has been known to send their chavlings into school with chicken pox, or some other such infectious condition, in order to get the essential freebie.

In the fifties there used to be school stories of jolly japes that inevitably involved a food fight. For the chavling of today, no such frivolity is likely to occur. Food in the chav household is at a far higher premium than it ever was in the days of rationing. There used to be a stigma attached to receiving free

Four reasons why a chav attends school (even as much as twice a week):

1. **They're bored with hanging around the shopping centres.**

2. **They're fed up dodging the police.**

3. **Mum has said that if she's up in court because of non-attendance one more time she will 'do 'em in'.**

4. **They want to piss off the other kids at school.**

school meals and some poorer families would send their kids in with a packed lunch rather than accept such a benefit. However, as the balance has shifted in schools and many of the pupils now come from a chav background, getting the free meal is *de rigueur.* Non-chav children are now embarrassed to pay for a meal, and may be set about as the 'posh kid' if they do.

Chavs and Homework... In years gone by it was noted that homework would be done either on the bus on the way to school or in the playground on the way to the lesson. Nowadays, homework is binned on the way *out* of the lesson or ignored entirely. One reason for not doing homework is that if you actually do it you might look as if you were trying to achieve or learn something (which is a no-no in all areas of chav society). The most important reason for *not* doing it, however, is that you can't be *made* to do it by the teacher. This gives the chavling another good opportunity to remind the teacher of their unique power. After all, if you can totally disrupt every class you

*

Nowadays, homework is binned on the way out of the lesson.

*

attend and then fail all your exams, that will *really* show the teacher up, eh?!

Registration... This is the time every morning when all the amazing chavling names (*see* Name Your Chav Baby) will be read out at once. So, if you want to know which footballers and pop stars were famous five years ago, then just sit in on registration at any Reception class. If a child has a simple or dull name – say David or Susan – they will be stared at, laughed at and generally ridiculed – and it's very likely that Jamilla and Chantelle won't have a clue how to pronounce these names anyway! As the chavlings grow, this will also be the time to make your presence felt with a little audience partici-pation. As each name is read out the wittiest chavling will feel duty bound to shout out

various abusive terms such as 'bender' or 'slag'. And if they can find something even remotely amusing about a part-icular name then this too will be repeated as loudly as possible... e-v-e-r-y s-i-n-g-l-e d-a-y!

The School Toilets... This is one of the school's most important places, but it's a strictly no-go area for most teachers. This is due not only to the acts that take place here but also because most chav kids think it is amusing to *not* flush the toilets unless another child's head is shoved down it. In fact, school toilets will seldom be used for the more traditional functions, but will provide a great

place to smoke, threaten other children and buy and sell illegal items. They also serve as valuable 'community' noticeboards where important information can be posted:

for sex with
Brandi call
07722 8*39*8

But we shouldn't just view these places as trouble spots. They can offer the chav child a great opportunity to practise their own unique kind of vocational or academic training course: Plumbing for Beginners (removing sinks, fixtures and fittings); Physics (discovering how long a blocked toilet takes to overflow in comparison to a sink); Art (developing one's own unique graffiti 'signature' using as many spray-can colours as possible).

*

School toilets provide a great place to smoke, threaten other children and buy and sell illegal items.

*

The School Outing... In a valiant attempt to give the kids a wider view of the world, the school will organize school trips. These will occur roughly every five years, which is just enough time to allow the staff to recover from the breakdowns they suffered after all the horrors that took place during the previous school journey.

The organization of these trips will begin with the handing out of permission slips. It generally takes about two months for the pupils to return the slips, which they will lose several times, and bring in the money. Even then there will be complaints about how much it costs and the almost inevitable, 'Whatever 'appened to free education?' debate. Finally the day will arrive and the teacher will try to get all the chavlings on the coach and to the destination in one piece. To achieve this they will need to run up and down the coach during the entire journey on the motorway as the quieter kids at the front of the coach compete in the school vomiting championships. (This, of course, allows everyone a unique opportunity to get a second view

*

The chavlings scrunched together at the back of the coach get the best view of other motorists who they taunt with obscene hand and 'quality' mooning-type gestures

*

of the bubblegum-flavoured drinks and orange crisps consumed earlier.) All the while, the 'bad' kids, who have commandeered the back seat, conduct their own vicious battles with each other. This group of fifteen chavlings scrunched together in a six-seater space, get the best view of other motorists who they taunt with obscene hand and 'quality' mooning-type gestures. The brave but misguided teacher will spend the rest of the day trying to round up the kids – although, frankly, if she can avoid the entire class being kicked out of the venue before 2 p.m., and can get the coach  driver to agree to return them to school, she will consider the trip to be an unqualified success. (If the coach returns with less than three missing children, this will be deemed to be an 'acceptable' rate of return.)

Parents' Evening...

The one place it is often hard to spot a chav is at Parents' Evening – but if you do spot one, it won't be hard to match the parents to the child. (The chavlings will look like 'mini me' versions of their parents – grubby and gormless.) Although chav parents know just how badly behaved their offspring are, they have no desire to hear about it from some snobby teacher. But if they do stick around long enough to hear anything untoward about li'l Billy Bob, they will stick up for him regardless of the evidence presented to them! Any reported bad behaviour will be, a) because of the other kids, b) because of the bad teachers, or c) because of the child's dyslexia/hyperactivity. And chav parents will *always* resolutely refuse to take the blame for anything. If there is any suggestion that they should or could do more to help their child's schooling, they will threaten to sue, 'take it to the papers' or contact *Watchdog*. They know their rights, even if they don't know how to spell them!

School Plays and Concerts...

Although chav parents have little interest in their offspring's formal education, they will usually turn up to any school event that their chavling might be involved in. They will also view the fact that their child is involved in such an event as a great celebration – and one that the entire extended family (including screaming babies) *must* attend.

The chavling's part in this event could be fairly minor – e.g. when they 'star' as the fifth hamster in the Nativity play, or the eighth triangle player at the school concert. The important thing for the chav to remember is that their kid is better than all the other kids, so they can talk when anyone else is doing something on stage. When their kid comes on stage, they must whoop and holler for all they're worth. If they're especially proud of their kid, but have relatives that couldn't attend, they will text-message them or phone and report on the performance as it's happening so that they can share their parental joy.

DEAD PROUD OF OUR KYLIE – SHES F**** GR8 ON STAGE

A typical chav learning curriculum consists of what they will need in order to:

1. write graffiti

2. fill out the claims direct forms

3. access the maximum amount of housing benefit

4. work out where value beans are cheapest

Tests and Exams... A chav will usually refuse to learn anything more than the basics (what they need in order to write graffiti, fill out the claims direct forms, access the maximum amount of housing benefit and work out where value beans are cheapest). But still, most of them are encouraged to study for and take exams that have little or no relevance to their futures, and will prove of no use to them even if they did pass them. Here's a rundown on the type of examination questions that might prove more useful and challenging to young chavs ...

ENGLISH LANGUAGE
Describe a place or a person you have met that made an impression on you. (This must be done in full TXT abbreviation. Marks will be deducted for correct spelling, accurate grammar and any sign of flair, but will be added for use of '8' and '2' and by coming in well under 160 characters.)

ENGLISH LITERATURE

Pick ONE question, but if you get bored then just skip to another or write something totally irrelevant.

1) Compare characters in *Pride and Prejudice* to characters in *Hollyoaks* or *Dawson's Creek*. (If you have not read *Pride and Prejudice* make something up or get the video out of the library. It's got that tasty bloke who was in *Bridget Jones's Diary* in it.)

> or

2) Explain why the dilemma facing Shakespearean characters, such as Hamlet and Othello, is not as pertinent as the characters in *Dude Where's My Car?* (Make reference to guilt, madness and passion and the effects of waking up drunk with random tattoos and losing your car.)

Jane Austen?
Dat's a bleedin'
***car** innit?*

GEOGRAPHY

1) Explain why the rain forests may be important to the Eco system but they are well boring and full of horrible bugs.

> or

2) Try to draw a map of the world, taking into account that the only two countries that matter are England and America. (Extra marks added for correct placement of Alicante and Tenerife.)

HISTORY

1) Look at the political climate of Russia before the 1917 Revolution and the relationship between the tsars and the communists.

or

2) Give an accurate account of the last three partners you have slept with and who they have slept with in the past three years and their relationships to each other. (Mention who asked who out and why they split up.)

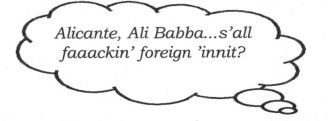

Alicante, Ali Babba...s'all faaackin' foreign 'innit?

MATHEMATICS

1) If you have £2.75 and you need to be able to sit in McDonald's all afternoon to kill some time, how many chips and drinks can you purchase and what is the ratio of time they must last you before you get asked to leave?

2) If you go into New Look and there are some well-wicked shoes costing £25 that are 25% off, is that a better offer than £5 off?

(Show these results in a graph. Don't worry too much about being accurate, but make sure all the colours look good and that you don't colour over the edges.)

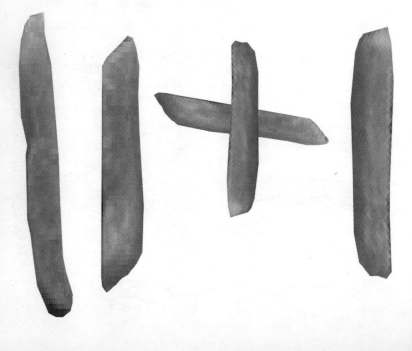

BIOLOGY

'Wayne shags Bianca, Sadie and Angie and produces the children Tiffany, Shayleen, Harley, Alfie, Archie and Kellie-Faye. Only Tiffany and Shayleen are recognized as Wayne's children, so what are the chances of Kellie-Faye dating Archie and producing the next generation of super slack-jawed chavsters?

Yes, a chav's schooldays can be the best days of their lives – probably because when you add up the amount of time they actually spend in school, it amounts to – quite literally – just that...days!

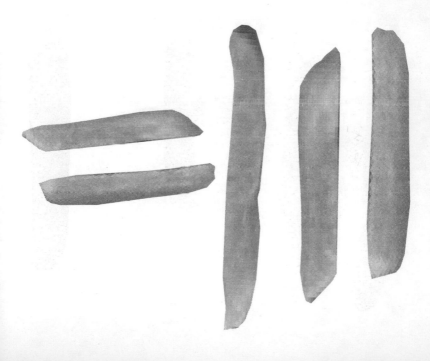

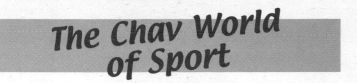

The Chav World of Sport

There are certain sports that chavs will get involved in – and those that they will avoid at all cost, such as snobby lacrosse, cricket, rugby, polo and badminton. No, a chav has but few sports to choose from: football, pool and darts. Basically, it's any activity that a pub might get involved in. Football is, of course, the game of choice and obsession. Chavs will pick a team, not based on its location, but purely on the fighting reputation of its fans.

As with so many other things, however, the chav will demonstrate his love for his sport through the clothes he wears and will purchase the obligatory footie shirt. This will be worn at all times and will usually be two sizes too big. Little does the chav seem to care that he has paid £35-plus for an itchy nylon shirt that will cause him to sweat like a pig, that has the name of some electronics company plastered

*

Chavs don't seem to care that they have paid £35-plus for an itchy nylon shirt that will cause them to sweat like a pig.

*

all over it, or that will be out of date within a matter of months.

For those chavs who don't frequent the grounds, there is one other option and that's the TV. So, whenever a big game is being shown on telly the streets and shopping centres will become chav-free zones. (You might spot a few straggling chavettes around who haven't quite realized that the way to attract a chav bloke is to feign an interest in the beautiful game.)

But if the streets are chav-free, the pubs are not and in order to ensure your own personal safety, it is advisable to make a note of kick-off times so that you can be securely tucked up indoors when the match finishes. This is when the chavs will be back on the streets, fuelled with drink. And whether their team has won or lost, it invariably turns into a lively (and often ugly) scene.

In the unlikely event that a chav finds the ambition

or energy to take up a sport as a profession, then it is likely to be football that he turns to. And as anyone who reads the tabloid press will know, most footballers are simply chavs with far too much money to spend. If the male chav abandons the 'weedy' look and piles on the pounds, he can go for the other favourite pastime: darts. To become a seriously good darts player a chav has to dedicate long hours in pubs (drinking), and needs to devour large plates of chips in order to be strong enough to carry the customized tungsten darts and the extraordinary amount of gold bling he absolutely *must* wear.

As far as the amateur playing of darts and pool is concerned, few if any organizational skills are required; these games usually just consist of one chav trying to show off his 'skills' to another chav and, like football, really only serve as an excuse for a fight. It's no coincidence that both these sports use equipment that can also double up as dangerous weapons in the wrong, boozed-up hands.

Even those chavs who have no interest in sport make an

*

To become a seriously good darts player a chav has to dedicate long hours in pubs (drinking).

*

✳

Whether their team has won or lost, it invariably turns into a lively (and often ugly) scene.

✳

exception when the national team is playing – the idea that they can show foreigners how crap they are is too much to resist. (If they thought they might win, a chav would happily get right behind the national tiddlywinks team.) To demonstrate their national pride and support for the team, they will hang flags out of the windows of their home and from their car aerials. These flags will then be left in place for several months and, tattered and filthy, will still be in place for the next major international event – which is handy.

Chavs will also pick on their foreign opponents' characteristics and subject them to endless ridicule. One way or another, they will ensure that they 'get it'. Kebab shop owners are usually in the front line for this kind of treatment in the post-pub world and will usually suffer if

England has been beaten. The exception to this rule is if the chav happens to live in a multicultural community, in which case they are likely to be confronted by a lot of non-Brits who are much bigger than they are. The blame will then conveniently be shifted to the team, the crap manager or both!

NB: as a rule, chavettes don't 'do' sport, unless you

✱

To demonstrate their national pride and support for the team, chavs will hang flags out of the windows of their home and from their car aerials.

✱

count the high-heel balancing act they try to perfect – or the evil stare that can kill at twenty paces.

Chav sports can be handily summarized by the old

Eng-er-land
Eng-er-land
Eng-er-land

Saturday teatime ITV show, *World of Sport*, which wasn't about a 'world of sport' at all, but just a bit of football, some darts and the wrestling. Today, this is the pattern chav sports fans invariably follow: a bit of sport followed by a bit of a grapple.

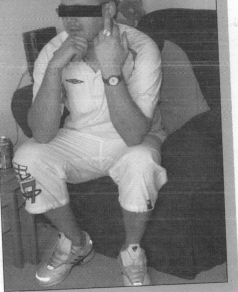

Chav TV Times

Why don't you switch off your television set and go and do something less boring instead? Yeah? Like what? As everyone knows, if a chav is indoors then the TV is going to be on. From dawn (about 9 a.m.) till the leccy runs out, the TV will be tuned in and, apart from short bursts of channel hopping through the 153 satellite channels, it will be tuned to ITV Chav, the channel of choice, where a chav knows they will never get stimulated or challenged or *anyfing*!

*

If a chav is indoors then the TV is going to be on from 9.00 a.m. till the leccy runs out.

*

Mornings are, of course, the jewel in the crown of the TV schedules and start with the pinnacle of a chav's daily viewing...the goddess-like Trisha. While others may make valiant attempts to tackle important political issues, ITV has realized that what a chav likes to see is other chavs fighting about paternity, arguing about who stole whose man and generally whingeing about how tough it is to live on benefits. This is a show for people who know that the best way to solve their personal problems is to play them out in public for the viewing scumsters and baying audience. Whatever the problem being discussed, you *just know* our hostess has had to deal with it in her own life...and she's come through all the stronger for her experiences!

> *Sharron – you are the weakest link... GOODBYE!*

Next on the agenda is *This Morning* – but with its slightly middle-class aspirations it can be a bit scary. (They talk about fashions that don't involve market stalls and recipes that don't involve tinned hot dogs or chips!) Therefore, most chavs will take this opportunity to check out Paaandland or nip out to buy some nice 9-carat bling at the jeweller's. Male chavs will use this time to pop down to the 'offie' for the first White Lightning of the day and top up their stash of fags.

After the dumbed-down lunchtime news (that will still prove to be as inaccessible as Proust to most chavs) and a bit of *Des and Mel*, chavs move on to *Pet Rescue* or *Murder She Wrote*. But this is also the optimum time of day to take a nap before picking up the chavlings from school (unless it slips their minds). And when they get back from the school scrum, there will be more exhausting chav choices to make. Will they go for *Richard and Judy* (a bit like *This Morning*, a little too demanding), *Countdown* (frankly scary) or *The Weakest Link* (eh? Wot?)? More often than not, chavs will opt for an hour-

FAMILY AFFAIRS

Dawson's Creek

long defection to Channel 4 because this is when they can settle down to watch that glorious duo *The Salon* and *Hollyoaks* (the one soap that chavsters dream about because it's 'so classy').

And before you know it, we're into early-evening viewing

Hollyoaks

Footballers' Wives

and settling down to the absolute staple TV fodder... *Eastenders*. Chavs love this soap because it speaks their language and relates to their world. And to make this easier, the BBC kindly invented the Slater family to

> *That 'aint a what-da-ya-callit for 'KWIZSHOW'!*

increase the range of chav faves even further. Like the Spice Girls before them, chavs have nicknames for each personality type: there's Slapper Slater, Mouthy Slater, Downtrodden Slater, Teen Slater and of course the queen mother and elder stateswoman of TV chavs – Old Trout Slater.

If a chav should ever miss an episode of this soap, they must promise to 'watch it on Sunday' or will be forever banished from the chav community.

Late evening will provide two chav choices. First there's Reality TV, along the lines of *Wife Swap, How Clean is Your House?* or *Holiday Showdown*. This will give them the chance to view similar filthy chavsters and laugh at them for being 'common' (they will of course see no irony in this). The second choice will be an 'ITV drama', i.e. *Footballers' Wives* or *Bad Girls*. The first is the ultimate

*

Chavs will watch TV endlessly, even the repeats.

*

chav fairytale, and will give them many opportunities to 'clock' clothes that they can look forward to buying daahn the market when the rip-offs arrive. This drama also provides lots of 'name your baby' ideas! *Bad Girls* is full of bitch slappings and lesbian romps and can, therefore, satisfy both the male and female chavster.

After this there may well be more attempts at news bulletins, so the chavs will have to drift in and out of family arguments, nod off to sleep and swig from cans of lager until the cycle starts up again with the glorious *Trisha*... Unless, of course, there's a late-night *Jerry Springer* on...

QU SW IZ

The Chav Movie Guide

To most people, the cinema is a haven of artistic expression, which uses all the technologies of the modern age to tell stories to enrich our lives, and a place for escapist entertainment and amusement. To a chav it's simply a place where you can go to start a fight, text your mates or snog your bint.

Of course, there are exceptions – favourite films that chavs would go out of their way to see. But because the average chav is unwilling to spend a fiver on something they don't know they are going to like, these favourites tend to be sequels. The idea of an original plot or idea is something to be feared not encouraged.

Refreshments are also important to chavs, and along with cans of Fanta and popcorn (which they will remember they don't actually like after about fifteen seconds and will then use as missiles, which they will aim at 'nerds and geeks' instead) most chavs will find it highly amusing to sneak in some alcohol. This is just another item on their checklist of anti-social behaviour aids.

In between texting absent friends and family (and even

*

To a chav the cinema is simply a place where you can go to start a fight, text your mates or snog your bint.

*

texting those friends and family who are sitting just two seats away) the assembled chavsters' fun will begin with the special feature, the merits of which will be discussed during the film like a running commentary. This is in case the rest of the audience aren't bright enough to grasp such important filmic nuances as the beauty and size of the leading actress's tits or how Vin Diesel is 'Da man' and could 'beat the s***' out of Arnie.

Of course, as we all know, chavs feel out of their depth in the outside world and so there is nothing they like better than to relax at home with a good movie. These movies will conform to the 'sequels are best' rule and the bloodier, more violent the film, the better. The heroes of these films, such as Jean-Claude Van Damme, Jet Li and the previously mentioned Vin Diesel are adored by chavs everywhere, and the likes of R&B stars such as 50 Cent,

*

After about 15 seconds, chavs will use their cans of unwanted fizzy drinks, as missiles, which they will aim at 'nerds and geeks' enjoying the movie.

*

Aaliyah or Ice T, are positively revered. When music heroes such as this are teamed up with kung fu fighting 'gods', chavs are barely able to contain themselves. Leaping up and down while they watch one violent episode after another, they're likely to proclaim this to be the 'best faaackin' film ever!' (A good example of this kind of film heaven is *Romeo Must Die*, starring Aaliyah, Jet Li and DMX. Any mention of the *Romeo and Juliet*-style plot will, of course, be ignored or met with a vacant, gormless stare.)

As much as the chav loves kung fu, other favourite genres include horror and sci-fi. Horror films must include as many killings as possible, all graphically rendered. And because subtlety isn't really a 'chav thing', psychological horror would have to be a horror film with a psycho in it – and preferably one who does all the gruesome killings!

TONIGHT'S FEATURE:

RETURN OF THE

BLOOD-THIRSTY, KUNG-FU KICKING, DIRTY-DANCING, ALIEN KILLERS 2

For sci-fi films to be a hit with chavs, they must be full of aliens – and they must all be (you guessed it) violent killers. Any attempt to explain the 'science' will be met with distrust and immediately labelled as boring. (Attempts to explain what was going on in *The Matrix* was only tolerated by some chavs because there was also lots of kick-arse kung fu action.)

Of course, female chavs like to look at moving pictures too, and as long as there aren't too many plot lines to confuse them, they're fairly easy to please. Their version of the straight-to-video 'faves' that their male counterparts adore are the 'Danielle Steele Presents' TV movies. These feature an interchangeable back drop (usually something like a New York fashion house) and will involve some sort of rags-to-riches saga with a nice

Any attempt to explain the 'science' in sci-fi will be immediately labelled as boring

and a nasty man that the female lead will manage to shag at various points during the plot. There might also be a missing mother or father. Any deviation from this plot line will leave the female chav feeling cheated. All-time-favourite female chav films will include *Pretty Woman*, *Titanic*, *Coyote Ugly*, *Grease* and *Dirty Dancing*. (The only new film they'd contemplate would be a sequel to any of the above.)

As chavs invade every aspect of modern culture, it helps to know your enemy and, when necessary, how to avoid them. For example, if you go to the local art house cinema to see a subtitled Bergman retrospective, it's likely that you will be able to enjoy a chav-free evening of entertainment. Unless, of course, they see the word 'Death' in the title and think they've stumbled on *Bill and Ted's Bogus Journey*.

Best faaackin' film ever!

Even betta than the first two!

Dear Shanice...

THE CHAV AGONY AUNT

Gotta Problem? Need Advice? Why not let the Chav Agony Aunt, Shanice, sort out all your worries...

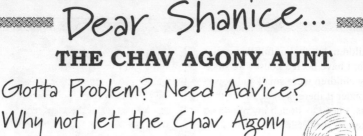

Dear Shanice,

My husband and I are newly married and started off happily, but for the past few weeks he doesn't seem to have any interest in me or anything I do. All he seems interested in is his work and colleagues. Can you suggest anything that I can do to put the spark back into our relationship before it's too late?
Henrietta, Hemel Hempstead

Dear Hen,

You might have a poncey name, but that don't mean you have to ponce about. I know what it's like when your bloke is only interested in 'is job. My Dave works as a buyer and seller of stuff he 'found' and is always in the pub selling it on. My advice is for you to go straight down to where he works and pull one of his colleagues. This will make him pay a bit of attention to you, and if it don't, then at least you'll 'ave a new bloke.

Dear Shanice,

I have been married for eighteen years and have two wonderful

children, but feel unfulfilled in my life. I have been a housewife since my children were small and now wonder if there is more to life than this. I need to stretch my mind and intellect further in order to feel like I have achieved something more in life than being just a wife and mother. What can you suggest?
Sharon, Luton

Dear Shazza

Eighteen years and two kids? No wonder you feel unfulfilled. No one can be expected to wake up to the same moosh in bed for that long, love! My advice to you is to leave 'im, find someone new and have a couple more kids. You won't have time to worry about anything with two more kids hanging about and causing you grief. And if you're still 'unfulfilled' after that then go back to 'im and split up again. Nothing like an on/off relationship to 'stretch the intellect'.

Dear Shanice

My boyfriend says he loves me and no one else, but I've noticed that when we go out to visit my family, he pays a lot of attention to my younger sister. I've always

thought she was prettier than me and I can't help my feelings of jealousy, even though he reassures me there is nothing going on. What can I do to make these insecurities go away?
Vicky, Beckenham

Dear Vic,

Look luv, this is right out of order. Go round your sister's and ask if she's after your bloke. If she says yes, then give her a black eye and pull out some of her hair. This will reassure you that she's not prettier than you. If she says no, I wouldn't believe her, and would knock her out anyway. You don't want to give her ideas. Also, this will make Christmas and other family gatherings a lot more interesting in future. Nothing like a long-standing family feud to keep things lively!

Dear Shanice,

I have had a best friend since we were children but a few years ago she got married and moved away. She now lives in a much better area than I do and only seems to phone me or visit when she has something new to boast about. I'm

sure she only does this to belittle me and it's really beginning to hurt. We used to be so close and I can't believe she has changed so much. What can I do?
 Beverley, Lewisham

Dear Bev,
Who does the mingin' bitch think she is? If I were you I'd go round there and dump a load of rubbish in her hoity-toity garden or start a good old slanging match on her posh new doorstep so that all her fancy neighbours will know what she's really like and where she comes from. That'll put her in her place! You can also tell her that her 'usband only married her cos he's an ugly git and couldn't get anyone better. That should fix the snooty cow.

Dear Shanice,
I'm in a real dilemma. My boyfriend has asked if I will have a threesome with him and one of his friends. I don't really want to do it but I'm afraid he will leave me if I refuse. What should I do?
Lucy, Croydon

Dear Luce,
First, ask him if it's a female friend. If it is, then tell him to piss off as that is bloody perverted, that is. If it's a bloke then find out who it is, and if he's half decent I'd go for it. Then you will always 'ave someone else to fall back on if your boyfriend pisses you off. If, after considering the pros and cons, you decide you're not interested in this set-up and he then leaves you, you'll know he wasn't worth all the aggro anyway. And don't forget to tell all his friends – in public – that he wanted to do it with another bloke. That'll sort 'im.

Dear Shanice,
I have three children and I don't seem to be able to control them. It's getting to the stage where I am embarrassed to take them out to shops or even to visit my friends and family as I don't know what to do when they misbehave. I love my children very much and want to be a good mum, but I'm at the end of my tether. How can I discipline them in a firm but caring way?
Nicola, Yeovil

Dear Nic

Hit them round the 'ed if they so much as put a foot out of line. People might look at you and even tut, but my response to them would be, 'mindyerownbusinessyounoseybloodycow' and that should put a stop to that. If this doesn't work and you still feel too embarrassed to take them anywhere, then don't. Let them play out in the street when you go out, and if they play up and cause trouble, then deny they're your children. This works well with neighbours and shopkeepers, but can be harder to pull off with social services and the police.

Dear Shanice,

It is my wedding anniversary soon and I would like to give my husband a wonderful dinner, but the problem is I can't cook. I want to show him how much I love him and I don't want him to think I'm a domestic disaster. What can I do? Linda, Dudley

Dear Lin,
As it's a special occasion, if I was you I'd take him down the pub. (And if you tell 'im you forgot your purse he can pay for it an' all!) They often do a nice pie and chips in the local. Don't, whatever you do, encourage him to go for anything too fancy or rich, or he might just get a taste for it. And you certainly don't wanna start all that cooking stuff! He might expect it every bloody year and before you know it, he'll expect you to hoover up and iron an' all sorts! Keep it simple, luv, and don't go giving him ideas!

The Essential Guide to Musical Chavs

If music be the food of love, play on…or if you are a chav, blast your neighbours with a moronic, 160-beats-per-minute bass-note for sixteen hours each day! Music is at the heart of many chavs' cultural existence – even if it's only the mobile 'music' of the polyphonic ringtones. It enriches their lives almost as much as cheap booze and fags. And when chavlings grow up – and move beyond the Top 40 pop singles – they branch out and start listening to three narrow genres of music: Rap, R&B and Dance. Keeping things simple and basic, chavs listen to Rap, chavettes listen to R&B, and Dance is enjoyed by both sexes. Chavs don't listen to any guitar-based music. Only 'grungers' and 'gofiks' listen to that stuff – and they are *all* freaks in the eyes of the chavsters.

*

If music be the food of love, blast your neighbours with a moronic, 160-beats-per-minute bass-note for sixteen hours each day.

*

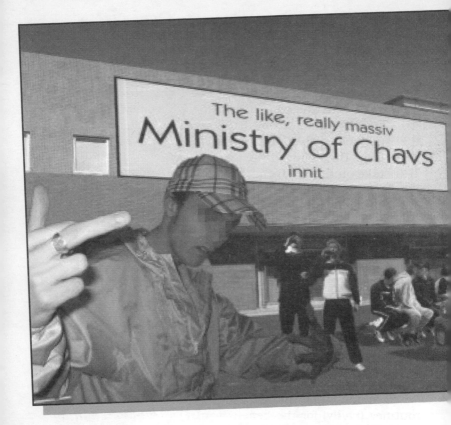

Rap... When they reach their teenage years, angry young chavs will tune into rap – and Gangsta Rap in particular. Lyrics that talk of LA street gangs, drive-by shootings, selling drugs and pimping encapsulate all the feelings of a sixteen-year-old chavster, regardless of whether he lives in town or country. And it won't be long before the young chav will ditch his middle-England accent and suddenly take on the voice and characteristics of his LA heroes. Listening to Gangsta Rap has to be an allmale affair. With all that testosterone coursing through their bodies, but unable to get laid *anywhere*, the chav, brimming with anger, pent-up emotions and sexual frustration, can identify with the misogynistic 'Bitches and Hos' lyrics of Gangsta Rap. But, blinged-up and snarling (as if ready to take on the world), what better place to listen to this – and share it with your entire community – than in the comfort of your own modified chavmobile, as you cruise up and down the local high street with your buddies.

R&B... If there's one way out of the ghetto for any self-respecting chavette, it's by becoming a R&B diva. Every chavette dreams of becoming the next Beyoncé, Christina or Mariah as they squawk their way through every Destiny's Child song at their local karaoke night and mimic their heroines' dance routines (badly) for the benefit of all assembled chavsters. With clichéd lyrics that talk of becoming 'stronger', 'tougher' and 'wiser' after breaking up with their man, the chavettes' songbook is the polar opposite of the misogynistic Rap music.

✳

It won't be long before the young chav will ditch his middle-England accent and suddenly take on the voice and characteristics of his LA heroes.

✳

Dance... This is the genre that is enjoyed by chavs and chavettes alike. Although the simple looped melodies and repetitive beats are perfect for the chavster brain, what chavs *really* enjoy are the more hardcore varieties of dance music: Trance, Happy Hardcore, Garage, Gabber and Drum 'n' Bass. This will make the chav think he is 'keeping it real', although he has no idea what that means.

Trance... The average chav's liking for this moronic dance genre usually has its roots in a vaguely spiritual experience the chav had in a field in the early nineties when listening to this type of music and 'ripped to the tits' on hallucinogenic love drugs. Having waved goodbye to millions of brain cells through the weekly use of Ecstasy and Speed for years, the chav now doesn't realize that normal people need to take drugs even to view this genre as music rather than just noise.

Happy Hardcore... Faster than Trance and relentlessly upbeat, this obscure genre is typically listened to by young teenage chavsters and played in bedrooms until, after several hours of torture, their mothers scream at them to 'turn it daaahn, will ya, Brooklyn!'

Garage... To the uninitiated, this is not a loose collective of chavs playing a form of dance music in their parents' garage. Oh no! Popularized by groups such as the So Solid Crew, this genre was briefly the chavs' preferred flavour of dance music. With its links to gun violence, it naturally appeals to the toy-town-gangsta-wannabe chavs and because it has its own female icon, in the form of So Solid Crew's Lisa Mafia, it is equally appealing to the chavettes.

Gabber... This is the most hardcore of hardcore dance genres and is only listened to by the almost brain-dead chavster. To normal people, this genre just sounds like an irritating fast banging noise. Just imagine listening to someone constantly hammering a nail into a wall, that's how bad this genre is. However, the filthy chav will think he is 'head strong' for listening to such 'hardcore choonige'.

✳

Just imagine listening to someone constantly hammering a nail into a wall, that's how bad the 'Gabber' genre is.

✳

Turn it daaahn, will ya, Brooklyn.

Drum 'n' bass... This genre, as the name suggests, is drum and bass orientated and is sometimes known as 'Jungle'. This was once a very much underground genre but when people like Goldie started to cross over into the mainstream, the chav then embraced drum 'n' bass. Although very much a flavour of the month that most chavs have little time for these

THUD
THUD
THUD

days, Drum 'n' Bass gigs can still be a right chav fest!

So, now you know what types of music chavs listen to, you can avoid the 'dance' isle in your local music shop. And when you hear that familiar 'thud thud thud' from an approaching car, just think of it as an air-raid warning and take cover!

Avoid the 'dance' isle in your local music shop.

What every chav wants as soon as they pass their driving test is a high-performance sports car to impress their mates (and the knickers off all the local chavettes!). Sadly, all they can afford is a fifteen-year-old Vauxhall Nova or Ford Orion that is one MOT away from the scrapyard. Which isn't a problem... The fact that the vehicle has one foot in the mechanical grave will not stop them from modifying it to make it look like a high-performance car. (We're using the term 'modifying' loosely here: what they actually do is 'gyp-up' or 'barry-up' their motors.) The first 'mod' a chav will make to their rust bucket is to fit a set of **Alloy Wheels**... Purchased from the local fence or stolen from another chav, the alloys make the chavmobile look like an old banger with a flash set of wheels on it. Which is why the second 'mod' must be made...the

fitting of a cheap and nasty **Body Kit**, the purpose of which is to not-so-subtly change the appearance of a standard road-going vehicle into one resembling a rally or racing car. Flared wheel arches, vented bonnet, the full works! And all that's now needed is to add some finishing touches to give the chavmobile that full-on 'cool, hard bastard' look...

- **fat chrome tailpipe** on the car's exhaust system to make it sound like the car is about to explode...

- **illegible number plates** – one with a fancy font that is only just readable...

- **blue neon windscreen-washer jet lights and blue neon under-car lighting** – to give you real presence outside the kebab shop at night...

- A really 'wicked innit' **ICE (in-car-entertainment) system**, one with stadium sound so that you can treat everyone within 300 yards to a sample of your favourite gansta rap, and a bass sub-woofer system so big that passengers and passers-by lose control of their bowels if a particularly deep note emanates from the speakers...

• **a spoiler** – the bigger the better, and preferably one that wouldn't look out of place on a Formula 1 racing car. (This increases the car's stability when cruising down the High Street at 15 m.p.h.)

• **the chavette** – yes, the ultimate accessory! Although having a wicked-looking chavmobile can bring untold joy, in order to reach god-like status in chav society, the young chav must team up with the chaviest chavette around – one who will follow you anywhere, pose seductively on the bonnet without scratching the pearlescent day-glo paintwork, and help test out the suspension day or night!

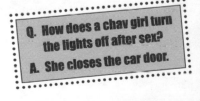

Q. How does a chav girl turn the lights off after sex?

A. She closes the car door.

The Cruise... When a chav has tarted up his rust bucket to perfection, he'll seek out his local 'cruise', where like-minded chavsters can check out each other's rust buckets. A cruise can happen anywhere, but the favoured locations are run-down seaside towns – such as Blackpool, Southend, Margate and Hastings. The meeting place for these events is usually the largest car park on the promenade or the car park of an out-of-town retail park (a much-favoured location as there will often be a McDonald's on site). Once they've been through the 'my flared wheel arches are bigger than the ones on your Nova' routine, they'll then decide on who's to be the King of the Cruise. (This is usually

*

The favoured locations for a chav cruise are run-down seaside towns.

*

the chav who's taken the most expensive unmodified car and, having added a tacky body kit and all manner of unnecessary bells and whistles, has devalued it beyond belief.) If you have a BMW or a Subaru you wish to destroy, you too could be King of the Cruise! When the cruisers are drunk and/or stoned enough, and the excitement has reached fever pitch, a bizarre ritual takes place.

*

Once they've been through the 'my flared wheel arches are bigger than the ones on your Nova' routine, they'll then decide on who's to be the King of the Cruise.

*

The cruisers will gather around as one driver after another seeks to ruin a perfectly good set of tyres by making the wheels of his chavmobile spin on the tarmac and smoke until they are almost burnt out. This is then greeted by a bizarre whooping noise from the overexcited crowd. And that, of course, is the moment when a concerned citizen calls the police. For a traffic cop, a cruise on his territory is like having his birthday and Christmas all rolled into one. Every chavster within a sixty-mile radius with an illegally modified car will probably be at this cruise along with a smattering of

A TYPICAL CRUISE GATHERING WILL USUALLY ADHERE TO THE FOLLOWING AGENDA:

- drivers compete to ruin a perfectly good set of tyres by making the wheels of his chavmobile spin on the tarmac and smoke until they are almost burnt out.

- bizarre whooping noise from the overexcited crowd.

- concerned citizen calls the police.

- police arrive – cue for sixty-odd cruisers to scuttle back home as quickly as possible.

- massive bottleneck of traffic created in rush.

- fleeing chavsters nicked.

local car criminals, all begging to be arrested! For those not too drunk to escape, the arrival of the police is a cue for the cruisers to scuttle back home as quickly as possible. Unfortunately this often causes a massive bottleneck of traffic – which helps the police to nick as many fleeing chavsters as possible! But isn't this all part of the fun of belonging to one of the most unique motoring clubs in the world?!

The Chav Guide to Wedded Bliss

Very occasionally a chav will not have a baby to Christen, or a new house to move into and yet will still want a party – a real knees-up with lots of food, drink and pressies. Fortunately, one of the unwritten rules in chav communities is that there is always at least one female member of any extended family who is 'gonna get married'. The male chav involved, however, is usually so gormless that he has no idea that he's due to be married until someone mentions the stag night. There will be no recollection of a proposal and if any mention of marriage was made, it will have occurred after the chavette has dropped heavy hints for months. These hints will be accompanied by tears, threats and tantrums, until the chav admits defeat and a cubic zirconia special is purchased for £19.99 from a catalogue or (an even a classier option) from 'some geezer down the pub' (which means it's 'hotter' than a branding iron). The male chav will never go down on one knee to propose, but this won't bother the chavette too much – she's generally realistic enough to know this kind of romantic gesture isn't on the cards and wouldn't want her man to be seen as 'poofy' or soft, anyway.

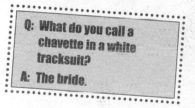

Q: What do you call a chavette in a white tracksuit?

A: The bride.

After the proposal, the real battle begins – the battle to win the title of Chief Bridesmaid. Bribes, threats and general cajoling will ensue, but this all counts for nothing as, traditionally, the bride chooses her ugliest, most ungainly female acquaintance and then puts her in a dress that will make her look like a pasty-faced heifer. (Anything and everything will be done to make the bride look as good as possible!) As for the role of Best Man, this will go to the groom's favourite drinking buddy and/or the mate who is most likely to make sure the stag night goes with a bang with the dirtiest strippers and/or local slappers in tow.

Working out the cost of the wedding will take up a considerable amount of time (and use up a considerable amount of brain cells). If the couple has recently 'come across' a dodgy credit card, or managed to blag a crisis loan, then no expense will be spared and the wedding will receive the full-on 'Posh and Becks' treatment. To chavs this is the ideal wedding and no amount of critical media coverage telling them that this kind of showy 'bling, bling' affair is tacky and tasteless will convince them otherwise. If a chav is slightly less well off, or is still paying off the CCJs (County Court Judgments), then the wedding will still go ahead, but with a few modifications. For example, the wedding licence will be purchased the morning before the wedding

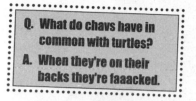

Q. What do chavs have in common with turtles?

A. When they're on their backs they're faaacked.

Despite no recollection of a proposal, the male chav will eventually admit defeat and get straight down to the bling shop for a classy £19.99-er.

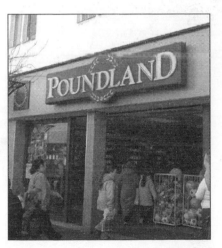

when the giro comes in, the flowers will be 'liberated' from the local park and a few throw-away snappy-snap cameras will be more than sufficient to capture the joyous moments of the day!

Generally, the catering will always be of the buffet variety as a full-on sit-down meal is far too intimidating for most chavs. (Sit-down meals at weddings are talked of in hushed tones and for the rest of their married lives, the misguided couple who attempted this elaborate nonsense will be referred to as 'Two-Forks'.)

*

The chav bride can take the simplest dress and customize it with more lace, feathers, bows, beads, ribbons and sequins than anything ever worn by a seventies Glam Rock band.

*

Either catering will be supplied by the pub hosting the reception, or the rest of the family will chip in and make their contributions the night before. Food poisoning is optional.

The slightly better-off chav might get a catering firm in to provide food they have never eaten before and can barely pronounce. However, they will always be able to boast about their 'canapés' (pronounced can-a-peas), 'pâté' (pattee) and vol-au-vents, which will be described by the guests as 'gruesome fluffy pastry fings with bits of green and white gunk inside'.

And then there's the dress: it is here that we cannot stereotype the chav bride. No one has any idea what she might wear, or what fashion style it will be cut in, but it will always be the most stunning creation never to grace a catwalk. In fact, the chav

Can-a-peas anyone?

bride can take the simplest dress and customize it with more lace, feathers, bows, beads, ribbons and sequins than anything ever worn by a seventies Glam Rock band. It will almost certainly have a deeply cut neckline, something that will allow maximum cleavage exposure to draw gasps of wonder from all who see it – including the vicar. (It is said that there is a competition going on among the chav brides: the first one to make a vicar keel over in shock wins a weekend break to Bognor.)

Before the big day, there are the hen and stag nights to enjoy – and for some they are the only reason for getting married in the first place. The hen night will usually be held in the local nightclub or, for the more adventurous, the local Greek taverna where all waiters can be grabbed and groped to the bride's content. The bride will always wear something really fetching for what is laughingly referred to as her last night of freedom – a tiny mini skirt, teamed with tiny cropped top, high white stiletto-heeled shoes and a sparkly veil. She'll also have a pair of L-plates slung around her neck and, encouraged by her mates who will be legless within minutes, will snog every man in the place and, without the slightest hesitation, reveal the saucy messages written on her thong to anyone who wants to see it!

Unusually, the male version of this hen-night hell is a far more innocent affair, and although final flings

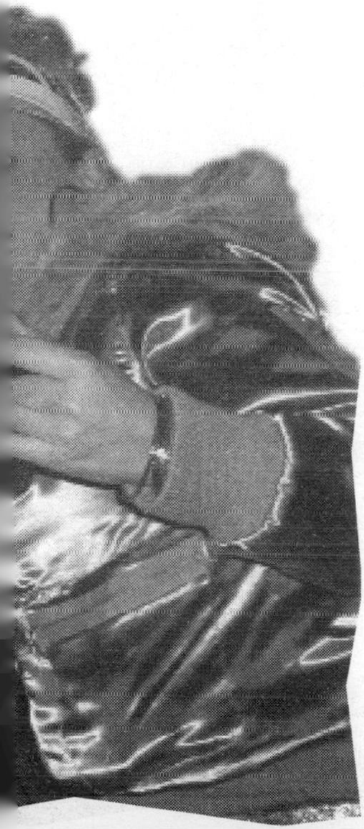

*

On the the hen night, the bride will be legless, will snog every man in the place and will reveal the saucy messages written on her thong to anyone who wants to see it.

*

will be much mentioned, the best man and all the other chav cronies will ensure that the groom consumes as much alcohol as possible and later, on the way back from the burger bar, will cover him in ketchup, kebab salad and tie him naked to a bin outside the local McDonald's.

*Well, it's me last faaackn' night 'o freedom, **innit!***

Finally, the big day – and in true chav style, it will be a day of tears and tantrums. In fact, if there isn't at least one good, entertaining fight then, according to chav etiquette, guests are allowed to take their gifts back. This, however, rarely happens because there is *always* at least one fight on the day and it usually involves a drunken brawl between the male members of the bride's family versus those from the groom's family. Or, if the bride and groom are from the same family, which is often the case, old family grievances are aired, usually resulting in one almighty punch-up!

If a fight ensues between the bride and either one of her bridesmaids and/or sisters, the wedding will be acclaimed worthy of a wedding-type Oscar. The canny bride that wants this type of action will always fling her bouquet towards the two female relatives

ON THE MALE VERSION OF THE HEN NIGHT, THE BEST MAN AND ALL THE OTHER CHAV CRONIES WILL ENSURE THAT THE GROOM:

A) consumes as much alcohol as possible

B) will get covered in ketchup and kebab salad

C) will be tied naked to a bin outside the local McDonald's

D) gets laid

most likely to kick off against each other or herself.

And then, before you know it, it's all over bar the bitching. The guests soon start taking

*

There is always at least one fight on the day and it usually involves a drunken brawl between the male members of the bride's family versus those from the groom's family.

*

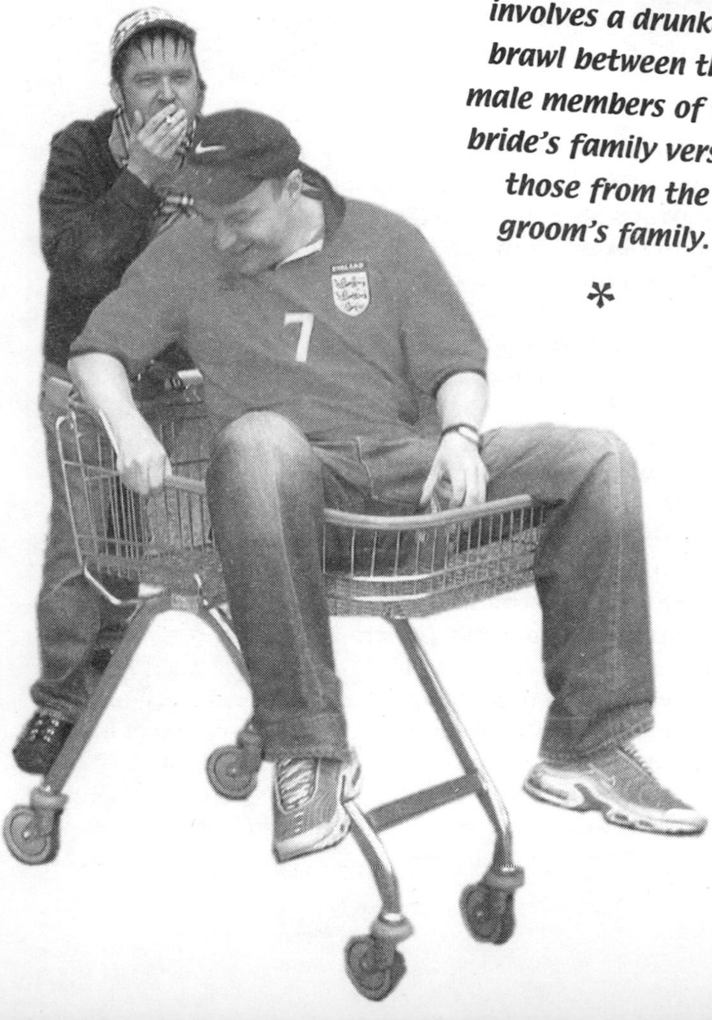

bets on how long it will last, and gossiping about the list of other people they *know* the bride and groom are still sleeping with!

And as for the honeymoon, this will usually be two weeks at a tacky all-inclusive resort in Spain, where the bride and groom will alternate between being rat-arsed drunk and sunburnt, or both, and will spend the rest of the time screaming at each other (but, on their return home, they'll tell everyone how 'romantic' it all was). Alternatively, the honeymoon won't happen at all because the couple have three kids at home who are so monstrous no one will babysit them for more than two hours.

Of course, we all know this entire exercise will be completely pointless, for it only takes an average of three months for chavs either to find other people to sleep with or to realize that, economically, they are better off on single person's benefit. Then they can decide to get a divorce (not so many parties or presents, but the opportunity for a good punch-up, which for a chav is nearly as good). And just like the pain of childbirth the chav will all too quickly forget about the misery and the drawbacks, and the wedding cycle can start up again. Oh, happy days!

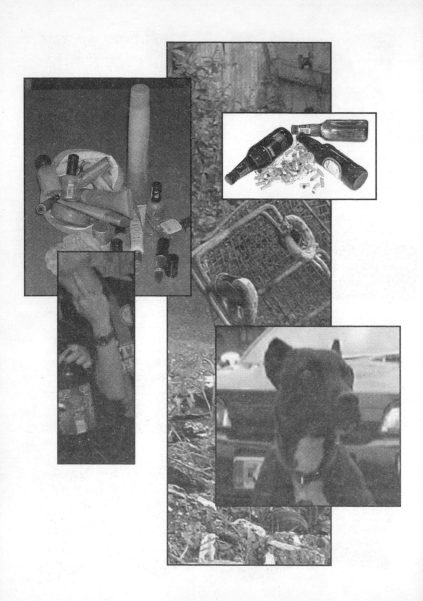

CHAV LIFESTYLE

The Chav Good-Grooming Guide

A chav's idea of personal hygiene and grooming will vary wildly from what most people might imagine is personal care, and there are usually two opposing schools of thought on this. The first is the 'well turned out' or **dapper chav**, and the second is the 'just turned out of bed/pub' or **slobbish chav**.

The place where the dapper and slobbish chav seem to meet is in the bathroom. Neither of them is big on washing, but the dapper chav will spend a fortune on perfume that can knock out a skunk at twenty paces, and can upon can of cheap deodorant will be used to mask any unpleasant odours. The slobbish chav simply avoids baths and doesn't care who knows it – or smells it.

Both types also seem to avoid dental care. But even if a chav takes relatively good care, most of his teeth will find their own escape route via fights or drunken slip-ups on the way home from the pub. The best way to sum up the teeth of the average chavster is that they are like the keys of a second-hand piano, one white, several black, and most missing.

*

The dapper chav will spend a fortune on perfume that can knock out a skunk at twenty paces.

*

Hair care is a vital part of the chav 'uniform' and for the female chav much will depend on whether she is going for the 'dapper' look or not. The dapper chavette will almost always have blond hair and it will always be scraped back off her face in a 'Romford Facelift'. And the crowning glory of this hairstyle will be the scrunchie, which will usually come in whatever pattern or material is fashionable that week.

The fake-Burberry scrunchie remains the classic look here. It is unrealistic to imagine this heavily coiffured style will stay up on its own, so added to the scrunchie will be mousse, gel, wax and whatever other hair product might be on a buy-one-get-one-free offer down the market that week. This look, depending on chemical components, will be either as greased up as a cross-Channel swimmer or as rock solid as Stonehenge. The dapper chavette will wash her hair every day. If she doesn't, her hairdo will turn into one of those sticky plastic wall-crawling spiders kids love to play with, and will attract every piece of dust, dirt and rubbish for miles around.

Mirror, mirror on the wall...

The male dapper chav will usually adhere to the same rules (with the addition of more Brylcreem than was used by the entire British army throughout the Second World War) but instead of the classic scraped-back style, he will often go for something more radical. One week this could be a 'parted with an axe' type of fringe or Eton crop, the next he'll be shaved as bald as is possible. But since the male chav will always finish off his look with his version of the scrunchie, the baseball cap, it really doesn't make much difference how he wears it. The slobbish chav's version of hair care is much quicker. They don't wash or cut it. If the need should arise for a cut (court appearance, forced Job Centre interview in order to stay on benefits) then they cut it in the same way as you would an overgrown lawn – a sort of half-arsed job that looks likes someone has lopped chunks off here and there with a blunt knife (which probably isn't too far from the truth).

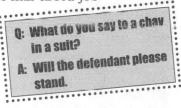

Q: What do you say to a chav in a suit?

A: Will the defendant please stand.

As mentioned, chav hair is almost always blond and if mother nature hasn't come up with the goods, there's always bleach. In order to maintain the essential chavster look, this process should never be attempted by anyone who might have any expertise in the field of hair care. It must always be done by a friend or family member at home (preferably in the kitchen) while the kids are running around and the dogs are barking. If other chavs hear you've been anywhere near a salon you'll be classed as a 'stuck-up cow with more money than sense', and will be burgled immediately.

The shade of blond the chav usually goes for can range from almost tangerine to a distinctly lime-type hue, but it will rarely look like anything remotely natural. For the dapper chav this is perfect proof that a great deal of effort has been made and serves to separate him from the slobbish chav who might also go for the bleach

FOUR CHAV STEPS TO LOOKING 'MINT':

FEMALE CHAVS

1. Apply half a ton of cheap make-up every morning.

2. Entice males with fake-Burberry scrunchie hairdo.

3. Bleach your hair for two-tone effect of faded greasy blond/greasy mousy-coloured hair.

4. Pop your pimples.

MALE CHAVS

1. Use cheap deodorant that can knock out a skunk at twenty paces.

2. Smother your hair with Brylcreem.

3. Wear dirty, dirty denim.

4. Pop your pimples too!

✳

Chav hair is almost always blond and if mother nature hasn't come up with the goods, there's always bleach.

✳

option in a moment of madness. However, once this madness passes and they realize that they 'don't do' grooming, they will leave it alone. After a few months they will have achieved a two-tone effect of faded greasy blond/greasy mousy-coloured hair.

The dapper chav will also aim for the bleached-out look in the denim part of their uniform. The bleached or stone-wash look will always be in fashion in chav culture, probably because with the need for bleaching their own or others' hair it really doesn't matter if they spill it down themselves. In fact, the slobbish chav doesn't care what they spill and will actively enjoy being able to look back on a week's menu, which has been saved for posterity on their clothing. They will also enjoy wearing 'dirty denim', but this is really just denim that has begun to rot from the inside out before anyone has even thought of it as a fashion statement. Indeed, since dirty denim became fashionable, we have seen the first appearances of dirty, dirty denim, which can often be observed to be so dirty it shines.

Skincare routines are an alien concept to both the dapper and slobbish chav – and since one cakes on half a ton of cheap make-up every morning and the other dodges soap, both camps are sure to have nice spotty complexions. This gives the chav two choices: to squeeze or not to squeeze. If the pimple-popping route is chosen, then the chav will be left with a series of

pockmarks
and craters that
even NASA would
think twice about landing
on. Alternatively, they go about
with yellowheads so juicy,
passers-by shield their faces at
the prospect of imminent
eruption.

So, as with most things, the
grooming techniques a chav
will employ will differ, but
really, no matter how long the chav has spent in front of
the mirror it will usually look as though they haven't
bothered. Which will come as a distinct shock to the
dapper chavs, who think they look 'mint', but no surprise
at all to the slob who couldn't care less anyway!

The Chav Good-Food Guide to Eating Out, Home Entertaining and Drink

Chavs like nothing better than eating out. In fact, because the very idea of cooking at home or eating *en famille* (with the exception of the summer 'barbie') is an alien concept to the average chav, most meals will be eaten on the 'hoof' and out of a polystyrene carton or a paper bag. And whether opting for burger, battered cod, fishcake or kebab, the one foodstuff that is always present at any meal is chips.

Now and again, however, chavs will push the boat out and go somewhere posh (any place that uses knives and forks will be considered posh), although going upmarket (Pizza Hut or Pizza Express) can create a few problems. Confronted by waiters, chavs will either be totally over-awed and subdued (which makes it difficult to take their order) or become feisty and aggressive in an attempt to show the waiter what's what.

But when chavs make the effort to eat out in restaurants (usually when the giros have just been cashed), they will drag every member of the extended family along –

including toddlers who are usually thrust into highchairs and then totally ignored for the duration of the meal, save for the occasional chip thrust into their sticky hands. The 'kid in the highchair' scenario is a common – and ugly – phenomenon. Not only will the child in question have no idea about table manners (like the rest of the family), but it'll bawl throughout the meal and throw food around until a member of staff (not a member of the chav family) finds something – anything – to divert its attention. This something, is usually a balloon on a stick, which the child will use to prod and thump every passer-by, much to the amusement of Mummy, Granny, Auntie, Daddy, Uncle and the countless cousins in attendance.

The Home-from-Home... Of

course the one place where chavs feel 'like everybody knows your name, and they're always glad you came', will be the local McDonald's, or 'MaccyD's' as it's commonly known. Patronized by like-minded folk, these little home-from-homes offer everything a chav is ever likely to need on

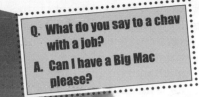

Q. What do you say to a chav with a job?

A. Can I have a Big Mac please?

the food and drink front. And although the recent introduction of healthy 'green, salady stuff' (something every self-respecting chav will resolutely refuse to order) has been a little worrying, this is one place where chavs know there's always a nice little squabble or two to listen in on, and no one stands on ceremony – which is how chavs like it.

The Outdoor Stall or Van... This is another place where chavs feel quite at home. It is the British version of the American drive-thru – and is known as the 'push thru', so named because when all the mummy chavs take their little chavlings out for a spot of shopping, they usually end up at one of these stalls so that they can give their li'l Chesney his daily fix of inedible greasy burger before making one last trip to 'Paaandland'. (The burgers served here will also cost a 'paaand' each; stall holders know that to deviate from this price – other than to charge an additional 20p for a manky slice of processed cheese – would cause a civil uprising.)

Another version of the burger van will be the chip shop, where any good chav mum can, after a hard working day of watching *Trisha* and arguing with the neighbours, give her brats a 'paaand' each, safe in the knowledge that they can get a bag full of sausage 'n' chips, saveloy 'n' chips or even meat 'n' chips. The

Noffink wrong wit' a burgaa now and then!

'meat' in question here will be kebab meat, which has been designed purely for the chav by the cunning takeaway owner who knows what his customers want and gives it to them – grease, grease and more grease, and absolutely nothing green or healthy. On the takeaway premises you will also find a flashing, sparkly fruit machine. These provide a handy distraction that stops the chavlings braying for their artery-clogging meals as they stuff 10p coins in the slots until the food arrives.

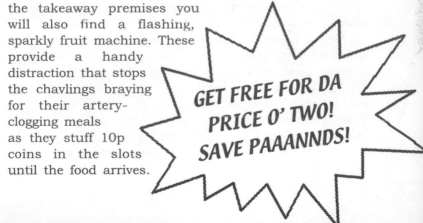

GET FREE FOR DA PRICE O' TWO! SAVE PAAANNDS!

There will be at least five chavlings fighting over the machine, all trying to win enough money so that li'l Jordan can have a meal of his own and won't have to make do with leftovers.

Home Cooking... Very, very

occasionally, if the chip shop is shut or the kitty is emptier than usual, a chav will try cooking at home. Chav mums will have seen many TV chefs, of course, although they will only remember 'that nice Ainsley 'Aarriott'. (They're deeply suspicious of that Jamie Oliver, who they suspect isn't quite as much of a 'geezer' as he makes out!) Inspired by the culinary delights they've seen, they will dream of concocting a delicious and nutritious gastronomic masterpiece. Of course, what they end up with is value sausages and chips or crispy pancakes and chips. The crispy pancake is a unique foodstuff that resembles a minced beef and onion pie, but is far more exciting as it's covered in day-glo breadcrumbs and packed with e-numbers. And of course, no self-respecting chav would be without their 9p-a-tin value beans or spaghetti hoops. (The little ones love putting these hoops on their ears as they mimic their mum's bling-bling earrings. *Bless*!) The lovely-looking value food labels – pretty blue and white stripy packaging – co-ordinate well in the cupboards, and because it costs far less than other foods, leaves more money for bling. This kind of consideration, as every

*

Any mention of anything even remotely 'foreign' like paprika, anchovies or oregano may well get you labelled as some kind of weirdo.

*

skinny rat boy or chavette knows, is far more important than satisfying violent hunger pangs or checking out nutritional values.

Conservative by nature, chavs are also afraid of anything that might assail their delicate taste buds, so any mention of anything even remotely 'foreign' like paprika, anchovies or oregano may well get you labelled as some kind of weirdo. And as a rule, fresh produce is limited to the humble potato (to make chips) and the basic banana (to shove down the throat of a baby not old enough to chow down on a burger while shopping). Anyone foolish enough to be found in possession of olive oil, sun-dried tomatoes or garlic will be marked down as a communist.

In fact, as far as chavs are concerned, food should be cheap, fast, simple and, whenever possible, prepared by someone else. Indeed, there is but one simple rule to follow on the food front: if you can put a 'Mc' in front of the name and it sounds plausible, it's probably OK. If you can't, don't go within ten feet of it. Example? The McSausage or McPie work fine, but the McArtichoke or the McLychee? Forget it.

DRINK! DRINK! DRINK!... Non-Alcoholic Beverages... It is a well-known fact the chavs are allergic to water. Being neither sweet nor alcoholic, any attempt to drink water will bring on an instant gag reflex and, very possibly, a vomiting fit. On the other hand...economy sugar-free lemonade and cola are must-have staples. Synthetically sweet and packed with an aftertaste that can turn the strongest non-chav stomach, these special-value drinks are like mother's milk to chavs. And certainly so much nicer than pure fruit juice, which is far too healthy and 'soft'. Fruit squash, on the other hand, is very acceptable,

Special-value drinks such as sugar-free lemonade and cola are like mother's milk to chavs

and another staple in the chav's store cupboard. Not only is this a 'cheap as chips' alternative to the favourite fizzy cola, it's prettier too. Packed with lots of lovely e-numbers, these value brands also ensure that little Storm or Charlene will be wonderfully hyperactive all day – and

most of the night.

But little chavs don't stay little for long, and before you know it they've discovered a taste for something a little stronger … Yes, the **Alcopop** (a.k.a. Slag Juice in chav circles),

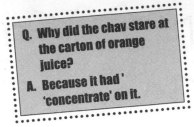

Q. Why did the chav stare at the carton of orange juice?

A. Because it had 'concentrate' on it.

which is an alcoholic 'training' drink for every young chavster, and conveniently ties into the chav's obsession with branding. Give it a cool-looking label, ensure that it

is electric blue or fuchsia pink in colour, and you have a winner on your hands! Until, that is, the chav discovers **Cider** – that all-time favourite with tramps and winos – or better still, depression-inducing Gin (a.k.a. mother's ruin). Always prone to tears, tantrums and violent outbursts, any bloke brave enough to ply his chavette with gin is only asking for trouble – or a hefty punch in the face! But trouble *really* kicks off when *her* 'fighting-fuel' is teamed up with *his* – **Lager**... When young chavs

I didn't ask for a Slag Juice!

graduate from drinking on the street corners or in their mates' bedrooms, to drinking 'daaahn the pub', the Alcopop is immediately abandoned (being deemed too 'gay-looking') in favour of the **Lager Top**. Although more palatable and sweeter than the 'neat' variety, once young chavs get a taste for the amber nectar, they soon progress to headier heights with a nice 'Nelson' (as in Nelson Mandela – Stella, the

✳

Trouble really kicks off when <u>her</u> 'fighting-fuel' is teamed up with <u>his</u> lager.

✳

lager also known as a 'spare room' in the more cultured chav circles).

Talking of cultured circles, at least once a week the chavette will seek out a more sophisticated

Q: What is a chavette's favourite wine?

A: 'I wanna blaaahdy go ta Bluewater!'

snifter, which means she'll opt for **Vodka** or **Wine** (white, fizzy, cheap and very, very sweet – a bit like your average chavette!). Indeed, many a Friday night will be happily spent swigging masses of the 99p-per-bottle variety in an attempt to get well tanked up before hitting a club. And if the wine and the lager don't do the trick, nothing gets chavs and chavettes plastered quicker than round upon round of sickly sweet **Liqueur Shots**. These can be consumed any time, any place, anywhere (again, a bit like a chavette) and because all sensible chavs know that it's not a good idea to drink on an empty stomach, they combine these with the new alcoholic jelly desserts – the perfect end to the perfect binge!

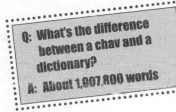

Q: What's the difference between a chav and a dictionary?

A: About 1,907,800 words

The Chav Guide to Mobile Mania

When a chav leaves the bosom of the family home and gets their own place, almost the first thing they do is get fixed up with a BT landline. Drunk with a sense of power and responsibility, they immediately run up a huge bill by phoning premium-rate lines and their mates' mobiles. Within six weeks, BT will have cut off their line for non-payment and blacklisted them with every credit agency in the land. The seriousness of this tricky situation will only dawn on the unsuspecting chav when they try for a contract mobile phone at their own address and will be promptly refused. Undeterred, however, they move on to...

• **step two:** reapply for a phone using the parents' address. Only problem here is that, nine times out of ten, this address is blacklisted too! Hmmm? Where to next?

• **step three:** the only form of communication now open to the chav is the pay-as-you-go mobile phone. Not so cool, granted, but if it keeps you in the mobile phone game, and you don't advertise the fact that you have to buy top-ups, you can just about get away with this without losing too much street cred.

Scrounge-as-you-go

Status... Many years ago, having a mobile phone was seen as a status symbol and to chavs, this is still very much the case. Chavs will try to display their mobiles at all times to gain respect from other chavs. The flasher and newer the phone is, the higher a chav's position in the chav hierarchy. As with most things chav, visibility is everything; you may have noticed how some chavs even wear their mobiles like pendants – which is not only uncomfortable and cumbersome, but an open invitation to muggers. However, either this has not dawned on young chavs or they simply don't care; advertising the new prize possession is all that matters. (One Chatham chav was once overhead saying, 'Look at me new "Nokyer"! It's faaakin' lush, innit?')

Expense... One of the things a chav will learn as soon as they get their first mobile is that they actually can't afford to call anyone. 'I'm aaahta cred-it' is the all too familiar cry. They will therefore use text messaging at every available opportunity, usually sending a text message to someone to call them! Some of the more filthy chavs

Im aaahta cred8 moosh

have also learnt a cunning trick, which is based on that age-old human characteristic, curiosity. Using Caller ID to their advantage when phoning strangers or businesses, it works like this: the chav will call the person, let the phone ring a few times and then hang up or hang up as soon as the phone is answered. Naturally the person they are calling thinks they have missed a call and will dial the chav back using Caller ID, thus saving the chav the cost of a call!

Text Speak... Before the days of T9 predictive text and unlimited length text messages, chavs developed their own form of abbreviated English to write as much as they could with 168 characters. In its most basic form, Text Speak consists of removing vowels from a word and replacing parts of words with numbers to shorten a word, or a combination of the two. Also single letters are used instead of a whole word. For example:

```
U  = you
R  = are
C  = see
M8 = mate
L8r = later
```

Therefore the sentence 'Are you my mate? See you later!' would look like this in Text Speak: 'r u my m8?

**AAAHTA CRED-IT?
TRY USING CALLER ID.
HERE'S HOW IT WORKS:**

1. Phone a stranger.

2. Let the phone ring a few times and then hang up.

3. Wait for a few minutes until the person you are calling thinks they have missed a call and dials back using Caller ID.

4. Talk for ages as you're not paying for the call!

I'll Nokyer block off!

C u l8r!' The mobile phone industry thought that the introduction of predictive text messaging would see an end to Text Speak. However, mobile phone manufacturers did not take the under-educated chav into account when they introduced their cunning new plan. To use predictive text successfully, you have to know how to spell the word you want to write. Naturally, this is a big problem for the chav who's had a mobile phone from childhood but can't actually write a sentence in standard English at all. 'Aaah d'ya spell... *[insert a word with more than four letters]*?' is a cry often heard when a chav is texting a buddy! The chav will then store their bastardized version of the word in their phone, so they won't even have to think too hard next time around!

Brands... Just like the sportswear clothes they wear, chav brand loyalty extends to whichever mobile phone manufacturer they prefer. Through years of handed-down knowledge and handed-down phones, the chav phone of choice by far is the Nokia. To a chav this is like a familiar old friend who they know and love, and who won't

*

To a chav a 'Nokyer' is like a familiar old friend who they know and love.

*

go changing on them. Using pre-colour Nokia mobiles is almost an instinctive pattern of behaviour. And whilst there are lots of other stylish phones on the market, to chavs they are, to quote another Chatham chav, 'just crap and gay'.

But changes are afoot – changes that might be interpreted as dangerous by some – because it looks like chavettes are starting to carve out their own identities on the mobile phone front. Yes, some chavettes are becoming more adventurous – rebellious even – and have started to buy Samsungs. Interestingly, while male chavs might like the look of these new toys, and they might even have the

occasional 'play' with one in the privacy of their own homes, they'd never allow themselves to be seen with one in public for fear of being ridiculed by their chav buddies for using a 'girl's phone'. They might even be branded a 'batty boy', which is the ultimate insult.

Removable Covers... Mobile phone manufacturers know their markets and that's why they make sure the lower end of their ranges are extremely customizable. Just as they do with their cars, chavs want their phones to stand out from the millions of others of the same model. And nothing else makes a chav's phone stand out more than an ill-fitting, generic, dodgy cover bought from the market. The male chav prefers phone covers detailing glamour models or cannabis leaves, while the chavette will plump for something pink and shiny, a Burberry-style check or Louis Vuitton-style pattern. Anything, in fact, that's going to give it that essential touch of high glamour and designer appeal!

✳

Nothing makes a chav's phone stand out more than an ill-fitting, generic, dodgy cover bought from the market.

✳

Ringtones... No chav phone would be complete without an up-to-the-minute customized ringtone, which provides hours of mindless amusement. No true chav would ever opt for one of the freebie ringtones provided by the phone manufacturer. If they did they

*

The male chav prefers phone covers detailing glamour models or cannabis leaves.

*

would be the victim of endless abuse and a laughing stock in their community. No, for maximum kudos, a male chav *must* have the latest rap hit for their ringtone and for the chavette, the latest R&B hit.

Many happy hours can be spent comparing ringtones – and in order to maximize their pleasure, chavs will usually indulge themselves in public places (buses, trains, doctors' surgeries – anywhere that will give as many people as possible the chance to tune into this ringtone heaven). In fact, it is not

*

No true chav would ever opt for one of the freebie ringtones provided by the phone manufacturer.

*

uncommon to be on a train and hear, 'Oi! wad jah tink of vis one?', followed by little Chantelle's phone bleeping its way through a catchy rendition of 50 Cent's 'In da Club', in the seat behind!

To sum up, a chav without a mobile phone is like a fish without water. A mobile is essential to text little Britney to 'get 'er arse aaahta bed' when you can't be bothered to climb the stairs or to secure that essential purchase of 'weed' for the next two days.

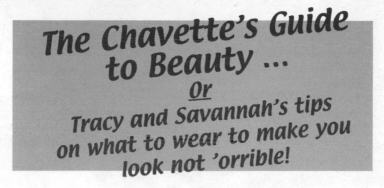

The Chavette's Guide to Beauty ...
Or
Tracy and Savannah's tips on what to wear to make you look not 'orrible!

As current fashion icons and girls about town we are often asked for our advice on what will make you look good, and we *always* try to help out. It's not cos we really want to make girls look any better, but cos it's something we can do and they can't, so we get to feel a bit cleverer than they are.

The first thing you 'ave to do is find out what body shape you are, see what colours suit or don't suit you, and then totally ignore all that and wear whatever is cheapest and brightest on sale down the market. We always say to people, take the 'magpie' approach to shopping and just buy anything that has the most bling on it. And remember, you can always add more. Too many accessories is just *not* possible. And if you buy from down the market and the bling drops off after three washes then don't worry. If things look a bit manky just dress them up a bit – or team them up with a nice pair of leggings, trackie bottoms or a baggy T-shirt and wear it around the 'ouse. If your jeans that had 'England' written across the bum, but now just say 'gland', then that can work too, so don't fret. The important thing is to make

*

Wear whatever is cheapest and brightest on sale down the market.

*

that style statement totally personal, while at the same time aim for an almost identical wardrobe as everyone else down your road. Don't forget, no matter what you wear if you team it with a 'wha'thefaaackyoulookin'at?' smile then you can wear anything you like.

Of course it don't really matter what your clothes are like if your

✻

The first thing you need to do is to find a mate who will have done a couple of months' hairdresser's training.

✻

hair and face let you down. The first thing you need to do is to find a mate who will have done a couple of months' hairdresser's training, or has seen more than ten episodes of *The Salon*, which is enough to make a good stab at your hairdo. Some people will tell you it's all in the cut, but we'd have to say it's all in the bleach. You've spent at least £5.99 on the bleach or highlights, so make sure it looks as toxic as possible and then no one can possibly accuse

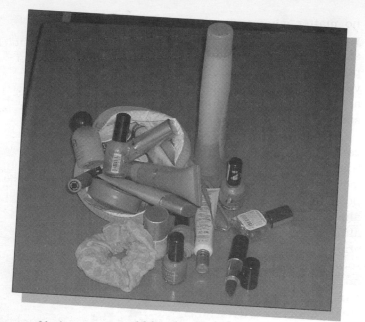

you of being a natural blonde. And if you do by any chance have a disaster and the dye goes anywhere near your roots, then be prepared to stay indoors for two months to allow full black-root re-growth or face public ridicule. For those of you who like the natural look, this is easy to achieve: just leave your hair to go as mother nature intended. For ever. The full-on greasy rat's tails should kick in after about a week and it's plain sailing from there. But remember

*

Pale, almost white eyes and lips will always contrast well with the orange fake tan

*

no matter what styling choices you make a good scrunchie should *always* be on hand to pull that hair back and stretch your eyes back so that you achieve that essential scary stare.

As far as make-up goes, you can either totally ignore it for that I-wanna-look-like-a-man look, or put as much on as is possible. Remember pale, almost white eyes and lips will always contrast well with the orange fake tan and the dark round the eye area and will in no way make you look like a panda who's just scoffed a cream doughnut. Remember too that you should accentuate all the hard work you have put in on the make-up side. Pluck out those eyebrows completely then pencil them back in very high so that you look permanently startled and insane. (A useful tip is to do this *after* the hair scraping, otherwise your face could entirely droop, and the Krusty the Clown look suits no one.)

We mentioned accessories before, but as we all know the

TRACY AND SAVANNAH'S TIPS TO LOOK T'RIFIC:

- Wear whatever is cheapest and brightest on sale down the market.

- Find a mate who will make a good stab at your hairdo.

- Stretch your eyes back so that you can achieve that essential scary stare.

- Put as much make-up on as possible.

- Use orange fake tan to contrast with pale eyes and lips.

- Pluck out those eyebrows completely then pencil them back in very high.

- Wear loads of bling.

*

Wear as many earrings as can be dangled on the ear.

*

most important accessories are jewellery – BLING. As many earrings as can be dangled on the ear and just as many chains, will look the biz. If these can contain some sort of cubic zirc, that's great – but it goes without saying that they *must* be made of 9-carat gold – and in the case of hoops, they *must* be hollow.

Of course this advice is all very well but it's good to have an example of who not to copy, and also of those

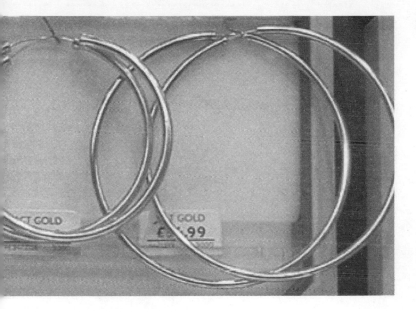

style icons who we'd wanna be if we could. So here's just a few of our classy babes and poor unfashionable gels who could do wiv a bit of help!

*Ah laav Cher – she's 9-carat faaackn' **gold** she is!*

Christina Aguilera

Raunchy, sexy, pierced and plastered in make-up, skinny wiv it; she's got the look, the attitude and the orange suntan! A chavette if ever there was one, and we luv 'er to bits!

Sarah Jessica Parker

Her telly show was good but her clothes were always just a bit too weird. And you don't wanna wear anything that would mark you out as a bit different, do you? Some of 'er shoes were OK, but not enough white stilettos for our liking. Course, when she started wearing them name-plate necklaces, you could tell she was at least trying to be fashionable in a chavish way.

Cher

We love her. Covers herself in bling and slap, lovely tarty outfits! She dresses like no one else on earth and you just know she'd give you a mouthful if you ever argued with her taste.

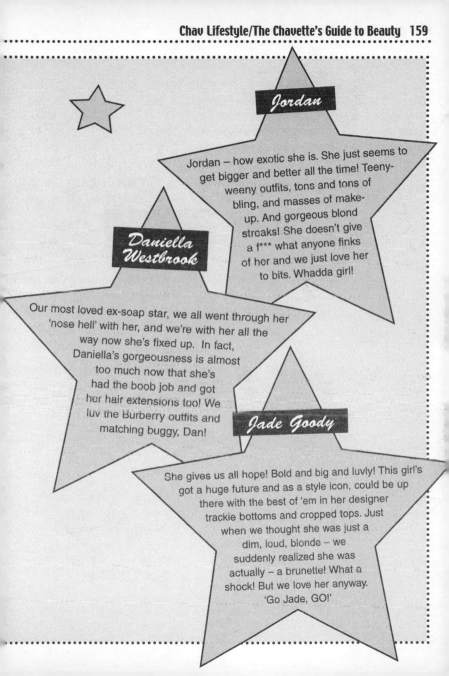

Jordan

Jordan – how exotic she is. She just seems to get bigger and better all the time! Teeny-weeny outfits, tons and tons of bling, and masses of make-up. And gorgeous blond streaks! She doesn't give a f*** what anyone finks of her and we just love her to bits. Whadda girl!

Daniella Westbrook

Our most loved ex-soap star, we all went through her 'nose hell' with her, and we're with her all the way now she's fixed up. In fact, Daniella's gorgeousness is almost too much now that she's had the boob job and got her hair extensions too! We luv the Burberry outfits and matching buggy, Dan!

Jade Goody

She gives us all hope! Bold and big and luvly! This girl's got a huge future and as a style icon, could be up there with the best of 'em in her designer trackie bottoms and cropped tops. Just when we thought she was just a dim, loud, blonde – we suddenly realized she was actually – a brunette! What a shock! But we love her anyway. 'Go Jade, GO!'

Atomic Kitten

Sadly no more as a group, but they were brilliant because everything you saw them wear would most definitely be in New Look or Mark One for less than a tenner in no time at all. Lots of nice fake tans, micro-minis and white stilettos! What more could you want?

Catherine Zeta Jones

Oh, she could be such a pretty girl, if she would just put a bit of brightness into that boring brown hair of hers. She might even be able to pull a bloke of her own age then!

Jessie Wallace

You can't get a better idol than this. She always looks well turned out and is at the forefront of chav fashion. Of course, she does have Walford market to shop in, which is a huge bonus. But we love the way everything she wears is tight, red, plastic and shiny – just the way we like it, and all so available in the local markets.

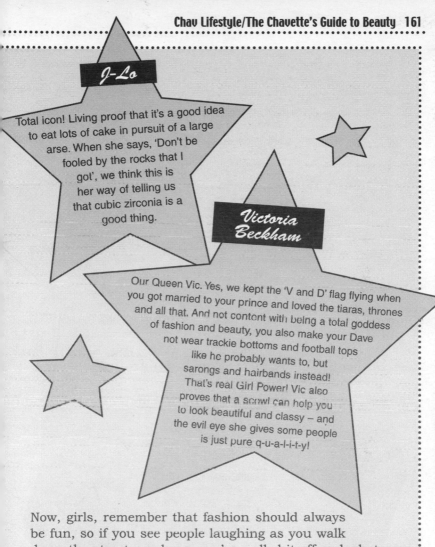

J-Lo

Total icon! Living proof that it's a good idea to eat lots of cake in pursuit of a large arse. When she says, 'Don't be fooled by the rocks that I got', we think this is her way of telling us that cubic zirconia is a good thing.

Victoria Beckham

Our Queen Vic. Yes, we kept the 'V and D' flag flying when you got married to your prince and loved the tiaras, thrones and all that. And not content with being a total goddess of fashion and beauty, you also make your Dave not wear trackie bottoms and football tops like he probably wants to, but sarongs and hairbands instead! That's real Girl Power! Vic also proves that a scowl can help you to look beautiful and classy – and the evil eye she gives some people is just pure q-u-a-l-i-t-y!

Now, girls, remember that fashion should always be fun, so if you see people laughing as you walk down the street you know you've pulled it off and whatever you're wearing has certainly worked. Mind you, if you think they're takin' the piss, you can always give 'em a good slap.

How Filthy is Your House?
The Chav Guide to Housework with Kelly and Maggie

The first thing we like to see upon entering a truly filthy chav house is an overflowing bin. The best way to keep the bin festering throughout the year is either to get yourself a large, slavering dog or to ensure that you block the bin men's way with a huge item, such as a rotting sofa or a broken-down old car. (If you put your rubbish outside in a wheelie bin and it gets taken away each week, you will be letting the side down. This unnecessary action could also provoke an abusive attack from your chav neighbours, so be warned.)

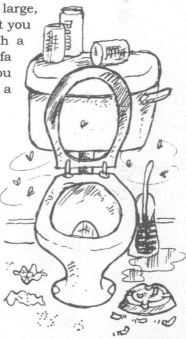

Once the rubbish has had a few weeks to fester, it should produce a large group of flies and maggots, but if this process isn't fast enough for you, not to worry. Take a leaf out of the chav housewife's book and chuck a few old nappies and some mouldy old kebabs on top of the heap. That should do the trick! And of course, if you did get a dog to keep the binmen from taking the rubbish, you will also end up with a few choice packages dotted about the place. And this is when you get the choice of either...

- picking them up and positioning them decoratively on top of the bin as part of the ongoing smelly bin ensemble you are creating

or ...

- leaving them where they are so that your entire family can tread them into the hallway carpet/lino all day long.

And don't forget, if you are a wildlife lover, then all the local tomcats can be encouraged to mark their territory on the front of your house and your street door. This will, of course, hugely enhance the bin smell, which should, with luck, permeate through the house.

*

If you encourage the local tomcats to mark their territory on the front of your house, this will hugely enhance the bin smell, which should permeate through the house.

*

And you really must encourage your cats to moult as much as possible (preferably over all soft furnishings, curtains and clothes), and prowl along kitchen work surfaces. If you can also train them to sleep on tea towels so that they become coated in hair, this is a wonderful bonus. Every time you use this cloth to dry a dish or your hands, you will be reminded of your furry little pal! And before we go any further, we must mention toilet training. It's important to remember that the little darlings will have accidents, no matter how hard you might train them to use next door's garden. (The same often goes for the children.) So do try to clean up after them, but never try too hard. If you do a really half-arsed job, the smell and the stain will remind you of your precious Tiddles long after her nine lives are up.

It's mingin' out there!

Returning to the chav-bin theme, you should aim to have overflowing bins dotted throughout the house. They don't need to be as much of a display feature as the wheelie bin outside, but a little time and effort goes a long way, and you can be as inventive as you like. Chips and crisp packets, frozen ready meals – even half-eaten dinners – all look good and add some colour to the average waste bin. If you have one with a lid in the kitchen, they should always be decorated, too. Beans, solidified fat and ketchup smeared across the top and dripping down the sides are, of course, classic markings.

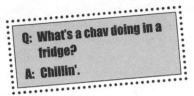

Q: What's a chav doing in a fridge?

A: Chillin'.

In the kitchen we must always remember hygiene and food safety. But since most of the food prepared by you in there is going to be bought in from the local kebab shop, we think you can probably forget all about these twin horrors. Ovens that are cleaned out will make the frozen pizza taste funny, and what good fridge doesn't have a salad box with a layer of unrecognizable goo in the bottom? Mouldy cheese? Not a problem – they charge *double* for that in some posh delis, dear! Grow your own and save money!

The bathroom is always a problem area and people wonder how their bathrooms compare to others.

Our advice here is just to make it look as though it's well used. But whether you use your bathroom once a day or once a week, as long as you manage to get dried toothpaste and soap scum splattered over everything in sight, and strategically position filthy, stained towels over every surface, including the floor, and leave empty shampoo bottles and rusty razors in the sink, then you're not going too far wrong!

As for the rest of the house, if you are going for that olde-worlde, classy look then a layer of dust is important and it's as easy as pie to achieve. Firstly, if you make sure you don't move anything about too much, a thick layer of dust will soon fall across everything and lend the room

*

Drinkers and smokers make a valuable contribution to having a filthy house.

*

that essential chic, dull look. A layer of dust also encourages the children's education, as they will always feel the need to write abusive messages if the dust layer is thick enough.

Finally, we would like to recognize the important contribution drinkers and smokers make to the filthy house. It's all very well giving up these pleasures for health reasons, dear, but let's not forget the wonderful displays that can be made from empty beer cans and bottles. And while a smoker can, over time, make all carpets, curtains and paintwork stink to high heaven and turn everything an interesting yellow colour that can't quite be matched on any paint chart, how much more delightful it is actually to see an overflowing ashtray in each room?

To sum up, dears, in order to achieve the essential I-can't-be-arsed-to-clean-anything look, you have to live the chav lifestyle every day. And if you're not prepared to put in the hours of slobbing about, then you'll never reap the wonderful rewards that come with living in a truly scummy, filthy house.

The Chav Day Out

A chav will usually stay within a radius of about one mile of their home. This could be because of the lack of transport, lack of finances or simply because they won't know where the chip shops are outside their local area. Occasionally, however, a chav will valiantly attempt something like a day out, or even some sort of holiday. These kind of chavs are known in the chav community as pioneers or great adventurers and will come back full of tales of strange lands...or, at the very least they will have mapped out the locations of strange chip shops.

A chav's favourite day out will be anywhere that's cheap, which is why you can sometimes spot chavs in museums or galleries. Another great advantage of going to such places is that chav parents know that the security staff in these places won't allow little Keanu to break the fingers off an ancient mummy, or let Alfie use a Bronze Age Urn as a spittoon. Like unpaid babysitters, they'll watch

Where's the chip shop 'raand 'ere then?

over the little chavlings – thus relieving the chav parents for most of the day so they can relax and have a fag outside.

Whilst at the museum, however, little Keanu and Tracey are likely to meet for the first time in their lives Tarquin and Jemima, the posh kids. Chav kids and posh kids will only ever meet in such places, and will be utterly shocked by each other. Tarquin and Jemima will thoughtfully look at the exhibits and pull out notebooks from their smart rucksacks, while Keanu and Tracey will laugh at the nudes (making a special point of identifying

all genitalia on display) and try to climb the carefully erected dinosaur bones. Tarquin and Jemima will ask Mummy and Daddy about the Aztecs; Keanu and Tracey will dodge yet another clip around the head as they're being pulled away from the fire extinguishers.

Another place where the chav kids can meet the posh kids is the theme park. The theme park is possibly the chav's favourite day out. (Not cheap, but the undernourished

Q: What do you call a chav on fire?

A: Blazin'.

kids can often be passed off as under-fives, usually until they are about eleven.) Here too, the kids can be let off the leash and, unless the parents answer the tannoy messages, they don't have to take control of them all day. The long queues that put other people off visiting these parks will not bother the chav. Unhindered by attempts to organize them, they'll usually behave so obnoxiously that the rest of the queue will collectively decide it's easier to let them push in front than to stand next to them for thirty minutes.

Blaaahdy **be'ave**, *you faaackin' animal!*

And while Keanu and Tracey happily bounce from ride to ride, and demand burgers, doughnuts and fizzy drinks, poor little Tarquin and Jemima can usually be spotted giddily puking into their sandwich boxes as Mummy and Daddy Posh regret attempting to mix with the proles.

*

If one of the animals poos or does anything deemed remotely 'rude', this results in screams of high-pitched laughter, and hours will be spent emulating the animal's actions.

*

Zoos and safari parks are also popular options for outings for both posh and chav kids and one of the places where their differences are most evident. Posh kids will have a favourite animal and will spend the day watching it and excitedly getting Mummy and Daddy to watch it, too. Chav kids will pronounce all animals boring, and will rattle the bars or bang on the Perspex enclosures until everyone in the zoo has fantasies about throwing the little chavlings to the tigers. The one exception is if one of the animals poos or does anything deemed remotely 'rude' (sexual), which results in screams of high-pitched laughter, and hours will be spent emulating the animal's actions. In fact, they might have been emulating the animals all day anyway, it's often hard to tell with chavlings.

On days out, the general consensus of what should be worn is split among the chav community, and goes from one extreme to another. One group believes that fleeces and trackie bottoms are the way to go for the entire family and they'll often purchase them in various colours, one for each family member. This may make them look like a bunch of Teletubbies but it also helps to distinguish members of the group when they're being rounded up like cattle at the end of the day.

The opposing school of thought on what to wear on these special occasions goes more for the 'we don't get out much, so let's wear all our best gear at once' approach. So, sparkly white trainers, white stilettos, micro mini skirts and literally *tons* of gold chains, earrings, nose studs and ankle bracelets will be in evidence. Again, all this bling clanking around helps to locate group members when it's time to head back to the estate.

If a chav can't make it to the theme park or zoo, they'll wait for the home-delivery option: the travelling fair. These are much like the theme parks, but filled with staff you wouldn't trust with the operation of a can opener, let alone a highly complex hydraulic ride! But it is here that

the chav girls can really dress up in all their best tat while their male counterparts demonstrate how hard they are by taking seventeen spins on the Waltzer after consuming about the same amount of beers. The 'hardest' male chav is the one who still has the contents of his stomach left after the contents of his pockets have gone. (However, since most chavs don't take more than £2.75 on any trip, this is not difficult.)

A picnic or day at the seaside is another nice, cheap option for holidaying chavs, and you can be sure that at any site there will be one or more chav families to spoil it

for everyone else. And, of course, they can't enjoy themselves unless the entire extended family comes too. The matriarch of the family will also have a voice like a fog horn that can pop glasses at twenty feet as she screams at her brood to 'blaaahdy be'ave'. This, of course, has no effect at all for every little chavling will be running riot within seconds of landing at the beauty spot. And if any one of them is unfortunate enough to be stung or bitten by an insect, they'll wail all day, or until Mummy Chav gives them a whack round the head to quieten them down. If the day out is at the beach then the older chavlings will smash every sandcastle in sight, steal ice-creams from baby chavlings and, of course, try to drown anyone foolish enough to step into the sea. Again, much wailing will ensue until heads are smacked!

A proper holiday is a rare treat for most chavs, who will generally refer to 'a holiday' as the one time

38 THE SUN, Friday, June 18, 2004

HALF PRICE!

they went anywhere and slept over. This will usually be in this country. Some unkind people have suggested that other countries have an embargo on chavs and don't allow them in. But it's much more likely that chavs have trouble filling out the passport application forms and would begrudge paying the fee anyway. The only exception to this is those chavs who have to go abroad to get the duty-free fags they can sell on to the rest of the housing estate.

Sometimes tabloid newspapers will run a promotion where fifteen family members can squeeze into a caravan on the Isle of Wight for a week. Such places will be run-down former holiday camps and will offer, as daytime amusement, a rusty swing park and a shop. At night-time, however, there will be a game of bingo and a bar in the club house, which will provide a real source of entertainment for chav dads. They can drink liver-rotting amounts of alcohol to block out the rest of the family, and Mum can spark up a

*

Sometimes tabloid newspapers will run a promotion where fifteen family members can squeeze into a caravan on a run-down former holiday camp.

*

*

A chav's ideal holiday will involve a game of bingo and a bar.

*

rivalry with the family in the next caravan over the kids, the noise they make or simply the 'funny looks' she's received from them all day. As ever, the kids can run around until they vomit or get a slap round the head – or both.

So, if you find yourself holidaying alongside chavsters, take a tip and join in *their* fun. Don't bite your tongue and try to keep your distance. It won't work. Just scream at your kids all day, drink gallons of beer all night – and don't forget the chips. You know it makes sense!

Two fat ladies – 88.

Dogs... A ferocious dog is at the heart of many a chav home. Dogs provide companionship and act as very good home-security systems.

The chav's pet of choice was traditionally the American Pit Bull Terrier. However, this breed did have a nasty habit of mauling the chav offspring, neighbours and postman! And given that you now can't get a Pit Bull because of the Dangerous Dogs Act, the chav breeds of choice are now the Staffordshire Bull Terrier, the English Bull Terrier and the Bull Mastiff. The truly filthy chavster will look for one of these breeds that has been crossed with a Pit Bull Terrier in order to own the most ferocious dog possible without falling foul of the Dangerous Dogs Act! To look really hard, chav dogs are kept on very short leads – the shorter the lead, the more ferocious-looking the dog!

Naturally, this dog will then fling itself with all its might at the chav's front door at the slightest sound from outside the house. This, of course, helps to advertise to the world that you have a vicious guard-dog and will prevent your neighbours' kids from burgling your residence when you nip out to the shop for some ciggies and a scratch card.

About once a week, a chav will feel the need to parade his best friend (dog) along with his partner through the local shopping centre. This is where he'll court admiring glances from other chavs, who will comment on what a fine-looking bitch he has. (Sometimes it's hard to know whether they're referring to the dog or the girlfriend.) For the dog, this little outing is great fun as it's likely to be the only regular exercise it gets, apart from when it occasionally escapes from the back yard to terrorize the neighbourhood. (It is also one of the rare occasions when the girlfriend will be seen out and about on the arm of her man,

✳

For the dog, a parade through the local shopping centre is great fun as it's likely to be the only regular exercise it gets.

✳

and tottering on her stilettos, she'll proudly strut her stuff for all she's worth.)

The chav will rarely bathe his dog, so invariably the dog will smell bad, *real* bad. This will give the chav house that distinctive rancid aroma of matted dog hair and sweat, which, when combined with soiled nappies and cigarette smoke, will assault your senses the moment you step over the threshold. Incidentally, if you do happen to find yourself in a chav home, don't be tempted to stroke the dog to placate either the chav or the animal. The dog's coat isn't shiny because it's healthy and well-groomed!

*Shaaadduuppp ya **bitch!***

And remember, chavs aren't into obedience classes. No, a chav's dog only has to understand one command from its owner, and that is 'Shaaadduuppp!' – which is usually delivered in a particularly aggressive and threatening manner.

EXOTICS... For a chav there is nothing quite like getting an exotic pet then looking after it...badly. Their favourite animals in this category are huge lizards, snakes and giant spiders. Convinced that they will make an excellent, cuddly pet, the chav 'must-have' lizard is the Iguana. But almost as soon as it's brought home, poor little Iggy will be kept in a cramped, unsuitable place and teased by the chavlings until it becomes spiteful towards all humans. It's only when Iggy has sunk its teeth into its chav owner or one of their chavlings for the hundredth time that they

✳

Chavs can have either a big snake or a venomous one.

✳

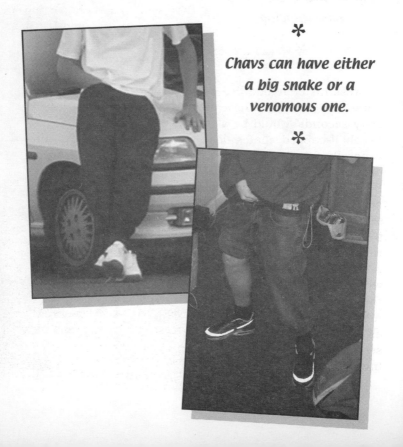

A chavette generally favours the large non-venomous snake, as handling one can be seen as an investment for a future career in pole dancing.

will give it away to the next-door neighbour, the local RSPCA or, if they can't be arsed, will let it loose in the back garden.

Chavs tend to fair better with **Snakes**, which are easier to look after than lizards. But with this species they have a choice: they can have either a big one or a venomous one. It tends to be the male chav who will keep a deadly, venomous snake, mostly to impress his chav buddies when they come round. 'Here's Fang, my pet viper...he can kill a man with one bite in sixty seconds' would be a typical exaggeration, while his baseball-capped mates look on in awe. The chavette generally favours the large, non-venomous snake, which can be handled without too much risk. (Owning one of these can also be seen as an investment for a future career in pole dancing.)

Monty the Burmese python will be fed dead rats while the chavette mates are visiting – which demonstrates to the assembled company just how fearless she is as she takes pleasure in seeing her friends squirm. Invariably, at some point

this snake will escape from its usual lair and the whole house will be turned upside down until the serpent is found. (It usually ends up hissing wildly under little Jordan's bed, just waiting to throttle the little monster in his sleep!)

Every so often a rumour will go round a chav community that the local pet shop has a **Tarantula**. This is another opportunity to demonstrate real macho bravery as the male chav enters the store and plucks up the courage to handle the arachnid. The feisty chav will then have a flash of brilliance as he realizes that if he keeps this spider as a pet, and if he can handle it in front of other visiting chavs and chavettes, he will be elevated in the chav hierarchy because of his bravery. He may even get the chance to mate with an alpha

✳

If he can handle a tarantula in front of his mates he will be elevated in the chav hierarchy because of his bravery.

✳

chavette. No contest, the purchase is made. Sadly, after just a few weeks, the chav will realize that having Winston as a pet has not had quite the desired effect: not only has he not been elevated into the upper echelons of his society, but he has had to come to terms with the fact that this spider is an extremely boring pet. Our disillusioned chav will not only have to take steps to sell the tarantula back to the pet shop – even if it means that he only gets half the price he originally paid for it – but will have to bear the brunt of malicious rumours about just how brave he isn't!

Cats... As we all know, the cat is the nation's favourite pet and fits in quite well with the chav lifestyle because they do not need to be exercised or fussed over too much. In fact, all they need is a regular supply of food – which, unfortunately, can cause a few problems for some chav owners. Because of their somewhat chaotic lifestyle, chav cat owners feed their moggies so irregularly that it often isn't long before the cuddly little kittens turn feral and begin to bring home all manner of snacks – from field mice to endangered species of waterfowl.

Another problem relates to contraception – an alien concept for all chavs, and

TIPS AND ADVANTAGES TO HAVING DIFFERENT TYPES OF CHAV PETS:

DOGS

TIP:
Get a dangerous looking one, keep it on a very short chain lead and don't exercise it

RESULT:
No more burglaries

SNAKES

TIP:
Get a big one, exaggerate it's venomous capabilities and feed it dead rats in front of your pals

RESULT:
Your chavette may discover her future career

TARANTULAS

TIP:
Handle it bravely in front of your 'gal

RESULT:
She'll be impressed and will want to have sex with you

one that extends to their pets. Chavs will rarely take the time and trouble to get their cats neutered, which means that the average chav moggy will soon be delivering an almost steady stream of little feral monsters – all of whom will be actively encouraged to crap in neighbouring gardens.

Some people say that owners start to resemble their pets and vice versa – and as far as behaviour patterns are concerned, this is certainly true of the chav cat owner. Therefore, a night on the tiles for a chav cat will closely

resemble that enjoyed by his owner. In his prime a chav has one main objective: to spread his seed as far and as wide as he can to produce as many chavlings as possible. For you're average chavette, a night on the tiles means attracting as many chavs as possible (which she does by mirroring the behaviour of most felines in heat, i.e. sticking her booty in the air and giving it a wiggle) in the hope that they will fight to establish who is the alpha chav. The victor then takes his prize...usually in any available toilet or in the back of a car. Needless to say, like their feline friends, chavs also feel very much at home in this situation in dark and smelly alleyways.

*

Some people say that owners start to resemble their pets and vice versa.

*

The Chavster's Guide to Gardening

To get the required look for a stunning chav garden the first thing you'll need to do is remove everything organic that isn't a weed. Chavs often worry about how they will get the weeds to grow over their gardens but frankly, once they get the rusting bike, supermarket trolley and old washing machine in place, everything seems to take shape quite effortlessly. Flowers and plants require time and effort and, as every chav knows, there just aren't enough hours in their busy day! Much easier to go for the dead-flower look. So buy the plants on a warm day in March and then plonk them straight in the ground without water or any further attention. This should provide you with nicely shrivelled-up flora and fauna in a matter of hours – which will, of course, look good and brown for the rest of the season.

A **Water Feature** will also help to create some interest. Now, some gardeners might suggest a fountain or a pond, but what's wrong with an old, slightly deflated, bright-blue paddling pool, complete with rancid water,

FOR THAT STUNNING CHAV GARDEN LOOK, YOU WILL NEED:

WATER FEATURE
(Old, bright paddling pool with rancid water and green slime)

BARBECUE
(Rusted to complement dirty white plastic chairs)

KIDS CLIMBING FRAME
(Rusted and unsecured to the ground)

OLD RUBBER TYRE
(Ideally suspended on a rope from a dead tree)

PLASTIC SLIDE
(Weathered, cracked and ready to shatter)

WILDLIFE
(Rats will be attracted by rubbish tossed directly into the garden)

CENTREPIECE
(Greasy old motorbike or mouldy sofa or mattress)

green slime and dead fish floating on the top?

And if you are going to use the chav garden for entertaining then you'll also need some seating and cooking equipment. A rotting, rusted **Barbecue** and dirty white plastic chairs should suffice here. If you buy them at the beginning of summer, they should have degenerated into their proper (grubby), more attractive chav state by about July. They can then be enjoyed for at least ten more years before they rot away completely.

The position of your 'barbie' in the chav garden is always crucial. Ideally it should be situated where it can have maximum effect – that is, where it can bellow smoke and waft the stench of charred 'value burgers' all over the neighbourhood.

To complement the entertainment for chav children, an old tyre suspended on a rope from a dead tree, a weathered, cracked **Plastic Slide** that is ten seconds away from shattering, or a **Rusty Climbing Frame** that hasn't been secured to the ground, will provide hours of fun for the children and more hours of fun in casualty for the grown-ups at the end of the party.

As everyone knows, **Wildlife** adds so much to a garden and if you throw most of your

*

If you throw most of your rubbish in the back of the garden you can be sure that you are doing your bit for conservation.

*

rubbish in the back of the garden you can be sure that you are doing your bit for conservation. Yes, the rats will be sure to visit your patch – although they may scare off all the livestock – such as birds and hedgehogs. They do have a dual purpose in that they can provide lots of entertainment for everyone when they watch them fight with the local cats that will be using the garden as a toilet or with the local scabby mongrel. Such fights can be both entertaining and educational, and can really add to the barbecue entertainment if you open a book on who the winner might be.

Every chav garden needs a **Centrepiece** – a kind of focal point – and it's here that you can really use your imagination. However, as that would require a lot of effort, it's probably best to go with a nice concrete ornament. Something like a life-sized Venus statue surrounded by a court of gnomes with red hats is sure to draw gasps of awe and wonder from all who view it. A sundial placed in

shadow can also be an imaginative design statement. If you are lucky enough to have a front garden, you really can't beat the **old-car-on-bricks** type of feature, which can be swapped with a **greasy old motorbike** or **mouldy sofa and mattress**, as the mood takes you.

Above all, it's most important to remember that gardening should be fun, and as long as your front garden can accommodate around fifteen of your friends and family on a summer evening, all swilling beer and shouting at passers-by, then you can't go far wrong! Happy gardening!

✳

As long as your garden can accommodate your friends and family on a summer evening, all swilling beer and shouting at passers-by, then you can't go far wrong!

✳

THE SEASONS
OF CHAV

The Seasons of Chav

As everyone knows, there are four seasons to enjoy each year. For chavs, there are but two: the height of summer or the depths of winter. As with everything else in their lives, chavs live with extremes and will not entertain the possibility of anything in between. So let's take a look at the seasonal changes that make up the day-to-day existence of chavs everywhere...

SUMMER... This is the chav's *most* favourite of the two seasons and also the time when they are more commonly seen out and about in all their glory. Like mosquitoes, when the sun shines, chavs swarm about and irritate the

*

Chavs like nothing better than playing the Boot Bounce game on a summer's evening.

*

hell out of everyone. This is particularly true of chavsters in the eight-to-sixteen age range, who like nothing better than playing the Boot/Bonnet/Boot Bounce game on a summer's evening. This daredevil game consists of bouncing along from one parked car to the next – denting, scratching and generally vandalizing the vehicles as much as possible in the process. (A bit sore on the bum, but great fun for these youngsters!)

Because of the heat, tempers can get a little frayed, so the summer is also the time when chavs most frequently bite, scratch and draw blood, and anyone unlucky enough to visit a casualty department on a hot day will notice that the place is full of bleeding (as opposed to bleedin') chavs. They are here after a day of drinking

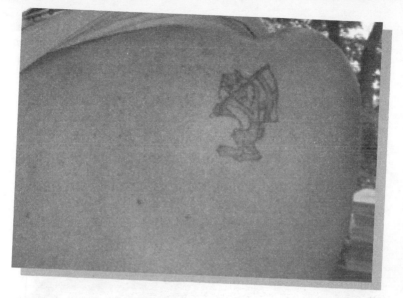

enough beer/vodka/White Lightning to bathe in, and have usually downed all this liquid whilst relaxing under a blisteringly hot sun wearing nothing but a pair of frayed England football shorts. Quite naturally, fights will start and blood will be spilled. The chav's Summer 'whites' tend, therefore, to be less of the cricket and more of the bandage variety.

In the summer, chavs will freshen up their homes, opening windows and doors for the first time in months. The unfortunate effect of this is that whatever horrors

✳

Summer is also the time when chavs most frequently bite, scratch and draw blood.

✳

have remained confined to the house during the winter months will then be able to escape. Pets and kids are, of course, the favourite and although the squawking cry of Ooo let the blaaahdy dogs aaaht? Oooooo? Ooooo? Oooo?' may never reach number one in the charts, it is a popular sound of summer all the same.

The clothing of choice during the chav summer will usually be something from their white wardrobe (hoodies, trackie bottoms, baseball caps and sparkling new

Ooo let the blaaahdy dogs aaaht? Ooooo? Ooooo? Oooo?

trainers) but the actual garment itself will vary, depending upon what the current favourite pop stars are wearing, and what is for sale in the local market. However, as far as chavettes go, they will always follow a simple set of regulations:

• <u>**Skirts:**</u> must be minuscule and the kind of thing most people would only wear after dark to the raunchiest of nightclubs. And, of course, they'll be about as wide as a belt and slung low on the hips to ensure that every stretch mark and tattoo is visible.

• <u>**Bra Tops:**</u> these will usually say something that is supposed to be cheeky and playful, but end up being quite truthful and insightful! For example, 'If You Think I'm a Bitch You Should See My Mum' or '99% bad girl'.

• <u>**Footwear:**</u> heels must be of the three-inch variety – but no need to worry about leather. In fact, plastic is so much in evidence, you could be forgiven for thinking that chavettes are making a positive statement on behalf of animal rights. Flip-flops are another favourite, particularly if teamed with a nice pair of very tight leggings. (The fatter the chavette, the tighter the leggings, needless to say!)

• <u>**Trackie Bottoms:**</u> like the bra tops, these will have a slogan emblazoned across the bum. It has been suggested this is a directive from Brussels so that the slightly dim chav male can see what he is letting himself in for when he starts dating the chavette who is 'Devilish' or 'Tasty'.

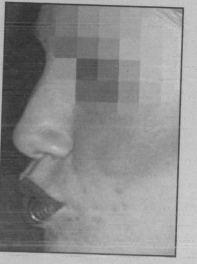

• <u>**Make-up:**</u> having paid no attention whatsoever to either school science classes or any of the common-sense guidance offered by beauty editors, the chavette will plaster her face in the thickest and most garishly coloured make-up known to man. In the heat of summer, this will of course melt and roll down her face almost as soon as it has been applied. She will then spend the rest of the day caking more on top of this sticky mess until she resembles something that has escaped from the circus. All the while, she'll be thinking she looks 'tops'. (This kind of foundation is multifunctional as it also provides a wonderful cover-up for all types of zits, blackheads and whiteheads.)

Whilst perspiration is a problem for everyone in summer, if a chav or chavette decides that the battle for freshness is not one they're prepared to take on, the rest of the community will suffer every time a slight breeze wafts from their general direction. However, the steps taken to mask any unpleasant chav-type odours are even worse. Clutching their 'paaands' firmly in their hands, they'll head off to the local market or 'paaandshop' in search of 'almost authentic' perfume and aftershave, with which

✳

For the male chav, the summer provides the ideal opportunity to show off a perfectly underdeveloped pigeon chest by the wearing of an unbuttoned shirt or no shirt at all.

✳

they will dowse themselves at every opportunity. The stench is second to none but can best be described as a unique kind of perfume that has rancid 'undernotes' of warm sweat and stale beer. Combining the aroma of chavs who have gone *au naturel* with those who have covered themselves in chemical scents is akin to being knocked out by a skunk and then being bombarded with smelling salts!

For the male of the species, the summer provides the ideal opportunity to show off a perfectly underdeveloped pigeon chest by the wearing of an unbuttoned shirt or no shirt at all. So, whether visiting the corner shop, supermarket, beach or Job Centre interview, the shirtless look is in evidence everywhere.

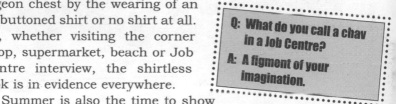

Q: What do you call a chav in a Job Centre?

A: A figment of your imagination.

Summer is also the time to show off (or get new) piercings and tattoos. Most of these will usually feature the name of most recent partner, offspring or dead grandparent. Working on the 'waste not, want not' principle, the more resourceful of the species will always try to cover up last year's partner's name with this year's – which usually results in an even more elaborate design feature.

Another popular trend in tattoos is to have the name written in another language. However, as chavs have little knowledge of the written word in English, and no knowledge at all of Japanese or ancient Sanskrit, they have to place their trust entirely with the tattooist. Needless to

say, there are some pretty disreputable types out there, and this has resulted in some unfortunate spelling mistakes. Since most of the tattooists' level of experience of Asian culture begins and ends with Chinese and Indian takeaways, it's very likely that the poor chav could well end up with a tattoo that he *thinks* says, 'Me Beffany', but actually says, 'sweet and sour pork'. (Which probably isn't a bad description of 'Me Beffany'.)

Piercings are another fun option for chavs and this is an area where they like to be as creative as possible. (They will usually have something pierced that shows how 'hard' they are – something that looks gruesome and which will appear to have caused a lot of pain.) A favourite with both male and female chavs is the nipple piercing. For the male they can show how much it bled. They will go about for days with a trail of blood running down their bare chest. For chavettes, their piercings can become little money spinners as they can charge the male chavs 50p a peek!

The most important of any chav 'look' remains the tan and both male and female chavs will begin to sit out in the open air from about St Valentine's Day in order to cultivate this look. The difference between the male and female chav is how brown they expect to be. The male chav will be proud and impressed if his skin tone changes from grey to white with a peeling rash of sunburn. The

female chav will settle for
nothing less than the deep mud
tones normally associated with blond LA babes. If the hot-
pants season is approaching and this depth of colour
simply isn't happening, the chavette will resort to the
bottle. Fake tan will provide that essential unhealthy
orange glow and, with luck, the streaky effect (which can
sometimes make her look like she's been fried in 'crisp 'n'
dry' cooking oil) won't be too noticeable.

But as soon as the weather heats up to a reasonable
level, chavs everywhere will declare the official
beginning of summer and celebrate with a

magnificent feast. They will call it a barbecue – and
everyone will know it's taking place by the thumping
drum 'n' bass as it bellows out from back gardens. (If
chavs don't own a loud enough sound system, they will
simply open all windows and doors, park their cars up on
the pavement outside their house and turn up the volume
on their car stereos.)

In order to feed the guests (only about seven usually, it just seems like more) they will need to go to the local supermarket and fill a trolley with enough beer to stock an off-licence, more buns, economy burgers and sausages than you'd need to feed an entire battalion and bits of chicken that are far too large to cook successfully over an open flame. So even if the giros have run out and they can't afford enough beer to fuel a really good fight (or if everyone is in a good mood for some strange reason) one or more of the party can still end up in hospital, albeit only with food poisoning. And since only mad chavs and Englishmen go out in the midday sun, this is about the time the chavs will begin their banquet.

The barbecue timescale will then follow this pattern:

12 noon: Barbecue lit

2.00 p.m.: Barbecue goes out for ninetieth time. All other males at barbecue will then have a go at relighting it until someone comes up with the idea of chucking some petrol on it.

2.27 p.m.: Nivea is applied to the scorched eyebrows of the bright spark (literally) who threw the petrol on the barbie – and all the men (and most of the women) retire with a soothing beer to help them get over the shock.

4.00 p.m.: The barbecue begins to heat up and the first piece of food is put on to cook.

4.11 p.m.: The first bit of food has turned to charcoal and has to be removed as it goes up in flames. It is then swiftly chucked over next door's fence, which causes much laughter.

5.22 p.m.: After several attempts, the first burger that is almost edible is slapped between a bap, coated in gluey, cheap tomato ketchup and offered to one of the 'starving' children. Unfortunately, the ketchup fails to disguise the worst of the charring and the child refuses to eat it. Despite her best efforts to coax the child into accepting this delicious morsel ('don't

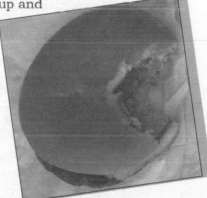

you know the black bits are the best bits?'), the mother accepts defeat. At least, she does until the child lets it slip that the reason he will not eat the burger is because he and his mates have been down the chip shop while they were waiting for the barbecue to be lit and are now full. This results in a swift clomp around the head.

6.07 p.m.: Even though no one is eating any of the food, it is still being cooked and there is now a large pile of black yet bloody meat sitting on a plate in the garden gathering flies.

6.09 p.m.: Someone has the bright idea to feed the food to the dog. The dog hasn't tasted anything as rich as meat in over three years and begins a barking and vomiting fit until someone throws it out in the street.

6.18 p.m.: The dog, due to its meat-crazed state, bites one of the children. Fortunately it isn't one of the neighbours' children so the police aren't called.

6.19 p.m.: Unfortunately, the bitten child happens to belong to the hostess's sister, who begins a tirade of abuse – blaming the hostess for everything that has gone wrong in her life in the past twenty years. This ranges from the dog bite to the 'sucking up to Mum for her money' conversation (which recurs at regular intervals) to 'accidentally' spilling her pina colada on her white shell suit and pink suede boots in 1986.

6.32 p.m.: The police are called.

For most people, the arrival of the police is like announcing the last dance at a wedding and a sign, therefore, for everyone to leave. For members of the chav community, this is the signal to merely decamp to the nearest casualty department, where the party can continue.

WINTER... As if afraid of the cold and damp, chavs are rarely spotted in winter. Like little creatures preparing for the long dark days, they appear to hibernate through this season. If you see a chav in your local McDonald's or KFC eating vast amounts of food, then don't worry. They're probably just stocking up for those long winter months. In fact, the only time they slip out of their 'caves' is when one of them has to venture out to the corner shop for ciggies and cider. And even for this short trip they will be bundled up in thick scarf, baseball cap, gloves, puffa jacket, fleecy hoodie and snow boots (every market trader's 'must have' fashion item).

But if there is one event that will draw the chav out of their lairs during this season, it is Christmas. In fact, to chavs, winter *is* Christmas...

The Chav Christmas

The season of goodwill and a time for kindness to our fellow man. Or to a chav, the time when you have a punch up in Woollies over a Transformer and a roll of Sellotape. Every year there seems to be a toy that children want above all others and while most parents will try their hardest to get it, the chav parent will pull out all the stops to make absolutely sure little Becky-Jayne gets the 'Dress me up, nail-salon, hair-bleaching Barbie' that she's just *got* to have. This isn't really due to the fact that the chav parent wants to ensure their chavling has everything they could ever want, but more because this, as with so many other things in the chav's life, is a contest that they *must* win. A chav will happily queue outside Toys-R-Us for four nights in order to get the last Orange Power Bear Ranger, simply because they can brag to the less fortunate (those unwilling to

*

Somehow the 'poncey colouring book and pencil set' is, to say the least, a considerable let-down

*

TOYS ⭐ CRAP

play this mindless game) that they've 'got the toy and you haven't'. This boastful announcement will be made in public as a sign of undying devotion to their chavling, but since it's the idea of beating other parents that's the appealing factor in this game, they won't shed too many

Goodness me.
You ARE cheap!

tears when it is smashed to smithereens on Boxing Day.

Chavs also like to take their little Weston to see Santa, but Santa likes it a whole lot less. When Jeremy and Tamsin come to see him they ask politely for the gifts they hope to get on Christmas morning. In stark contrast, when the chavlings come along they know only too well that Santa is just a bloke dressed up in a suit – and they don't even have to try to be polite to get their gift, 'cos that's included in the entrance fee, innit?' The gift, however, invariably disappoints. Believing they might be presented with some super-duper monster truck they spotted in the shopping centre on their way to Santa's Grotto,

On being presented with a really naff toy, the chavling may demonstrate his displeasure by swearing and kicking Santa in the shins

somehow the 'poncey colouring book and pencil set' is, to say the least, a considerable let-down. And not having been schooled in manners, the chavling will demonstrate his displeasure by swearing and kicking Santa in the shins, telling him exactly where he can stuff his pencils and then run off wailing in the general dircction of the car park.

Chavs enjoy shopping – even if they normally only bother with 'Paaandland' and the local corner shop – and they've discovered that three days before Christmas Eve is the best time to begin to shop for 'Chrissy pressies'. Perhaps because this is when the two weeks' giro comes in, or perhaps this is when they know they're going to get some last-minute, knock-down bargains.

Either way, chavs will be much in evidence in the shopping centres and will make a rare appearance at the local supermarket, which always results in a frantic scrum as they try to get stocked up with all the Christmas essentials, including things like bread sauce, cranberries, brandy butter and a whole pile of other 'nibbly bits' they've never eaten before and are unlikely ever to eat in the future. These 'must-have items' – which they've seen

Merry chrisssmas, moosh!

advertised at knock-down prices in one of the local freebie newspapers – will sit in the cupboard for the next decade, but that won't matter. At least they'll know they have them in case of emergencies or if they run out of tins of economy sausage and beans during the two-day Christmas shut-down. And if anyone gets in their way during this shopping expedition, they'll be in BIG trouble. Racing up and down aisles grabbing food blindly off the shelves, they will use their trolleys like ramming devices and, just for good measure, will let the kids run riot – which is, after all, part of the festive fun!

But not all chavs leave Christmas preparations until the last minute. Some are more than keen to demonstrate their willingness to take part in the season of goodwill and to ensure everyone knows this, they will begin to purchase tacky and garish models of evil-eyed, serial-killer-looking Santas around August. These will then be stored away until the beginning of October, which is, according to these eager-beaver chavs, the start of the festive season. They will then proceed to plaster the rooftops and walls of their terraced maisonette with at least fifteen Santas, seventy-four reindeers and a whole platoon of snowmen – and they will all have flashing lights which offer seasons greetings in 134 different languages. These national-grid-zapping displays will stay put until around February, by which time the displays often feature a headless Reindeer and a sign welcoming one and all to **santa's grot**.

Yes, for a chav the seasonal variations are simple. If the sun is shining it's summer and time to go out and chav it up a bit. Or else it's winter, and time to stay in and wait for the crates of Christmas spirit to arrive.

THE FOUR AGES
OF CHAV

The Four Ages of Chav

0-12 – The Chavlings

The arrival of a new chav in the pack is always something of an event, even though it is anything but rare. There is always much speculation about who the new baby looks like and later, in the pub, a lot of jolly banter about which one of the new mum's 'indiscretions' the baby most resembles. (Fuelled by lager, this situation can escalate into quite a tense and rowdy scene, which makes for a particularly lively welcome to the world for the new chavling.)

Children all develop at different rates and will do things when they are ready. Chavlings develop practical skills – such as walking, holding implements and fetching their own food as part of their survival techniques – from a very early age. Skills, such as talking sense and reading, come a lot later. This is partly because there is rarely anyone in the community who is willing or able to teach them, and partly because these things are not essential for an enriched chav life.

By the time chavlings are old enough to toddle, they can be spotted out on the streets sporting chocolate-covered grins and clothed only in grubby grey T-shirts and wet nappies. (In fact, there is a prime time when *Trisha* is on the box and just before *Teletubbies* start,

HOW TO SPOT A CHAVLING:

- chocolate-covered grin
- grubby grey T-shirt
- wet nappy
- gormless look
- sticky goo dripping from mouth

when chavlings almost take over the streets of most housing estates.) This period usually allows the chavling about twenty minutes of freedom before the ear-piercing screech of 'Get in the blaaahdy 'ouse, Chesney!' reverberates around the estate.

Chavlings, as we all know, tend to be blond, and the more pure bred a chavling the blonder it will be. (The lord and lady chavster of any estate will always produce a child so blond it is hard to tell whether it is a small but fast pensioner, or an albino midget.) After a few years, when the chavling has a few siblings to accompany him on family visits, the resulting gathering can look very scary – and not unlike a scene from

*Get in the **blaaahdy** 'ouse, Chesney!*

Village of the Damned. Not only will all the assembled chavlings have the characteristic slack-jawed, gormless look, but they will also have a large amount of drool and sticky goo dripping from their mouths. If you are ever invited into the chav community you may be required to give one of these mucky monsters a kiss. Unless you are prepared to blow your cover – which is inadvisable – it is best to deal with the situation fast; do not hesitate or think about the horror you face, just work out how soon you can get yourself – and your clothes – cleaned up!

Chavlings will *always* be unruly but their parents will

Most chavlings will simply laugh, stick a finger up in the air and continue on their merry way, causing havoc and damage wherever possible.

always label their demonic behaviour 'hyperactivity' (or whatever trendy condition has been recently discussed on *This Morning*). And they will blame this on bad schooling or an intolerance to Pot Noodles. In any conversation about behaviour, never ever mention the word 'discipline'. To the adult chav, discipline represents a slap, and there is no shortage of slaps in the chav household. But don't worry too much – the chavling soon develops a hide like an elephant – and the ability to dodge blows. Some chavlings, however, have the potential for obedience: if Mum's slap around the head catches nothing but thin air and she then beckons the little chav to come closer, the obedient chavling will approach without hesitation in order to receive the punishment. This is rare: most chavlings will simply laugh, stick two fingers up in the air and continue on their merry way, causing havoc and damage wherever possible.

The best place to observe chavlings is on the streets, for this is where they are most at home. Until about midnight a girl chavling can often be spotted happily playing with her baby dolls and pushing her pram up and down the pavements. It is only when you begin to marvel at how life-like the dollies are these days and take a closer look, that you realize that this is no doll; the chavling is actually looking after a grubby-looking younger sibling. There will also be frequent cat-fights. These fights, coupled with the pram-pushing games, represent invaluable early practice for what lies ahead for these young girls.

✻

Boy chavlings love to play football on a busy road packed with parked cars.

✻

Boy chavlings will *always* play football and when they wish to do this they won't bother to find a large expanse of ground or a park, they will simply choose a busy road packed with parked cars. Disregarding any thoughts of danger or road safety, a boy chavling thrives on this daredevil approach. He is like Captain Scarlet... indestructible. Happily running in front of cars, he causes as much chaos as possible and any driver who dares to challenge his behaviour will be subjected to endless abuse until the chavling legs it into the nearest chav house to find any available adult who might fancy a fight with the foolish motorist who, by now, will be regretting the fuss he's made!

13-15 – The Teenage Years

Adolescence – that bright awakening where a child begins to blossom into adulthood and grow into the person they want to be – for mini chavs represents a short period of time between the end of wanting to eat Popping Candy and the birth of their first child. During these years the chav will have to hang around in a group of at least nine or ten. Any less than this number is dangerous, for the mini chav is still at a vulnerable age and so can be picked off by a stronger predator or another group of mini chavs. Female mini chavs are, of course, exceptionally vulnerable. A single female mini chav will usually only last half an hour in a town centre before her ego is crushed beyond repair as her hair, her jewellery and her clothes are given the once-over by chav enemies who pronounce her look to be 'scummy', 'skanky' and 'from Oxfam'. This kind of treatment ensures that the mini-

chav pack mentality stays strong. Anyone brave enough, or foolish enough, to leave the group would, of course, also be subjected to the same kind of ugly abuse and scrutiny.

However, without an outsider to pick on, any member of the group – say someone who hasn't acquired this week's required bit of bling – may also become the victim of cruel taunts and severe criticism. In fact, they can easily become the 'whipping boy' for the day, and much enjoyment can be derived from making li'l Cher cry until she goes home to tell her mum.

Male mini chavs will also hang about in gangs, and will also weed out this week's weakest link – the group

*

A single female mini chav will usually only last half an hour in a town centre before her ego is crushed beyond repair as her hair, her jewellery and her clothes are given the once-over by chav enemies

*

Slapper!

member who hasn't quite come up to scratch. This victim will simply be pummelled in a 'friendly' way until he shows signs of bruising. But if he cries, he can never show his face in chav society again and may actually have to move house in order to avoid further humiliation and violence.

This kind of male bonding activity will usually take place in one of the mini chav's two hang-outs:

First, **The Swing Park** – originally intended for use by the little chavlings, these are always taken over by mini-chav gangs. Even

Scumbag!

when they can't be there in person, they mark their territory by pouring cans of cola down the slide and chaining up the swings so that kids can't reach them. The mini male chav will sit in these parks in all weathers and growl at anyone else who may want to enter. The exception, of course, being a group of female minis. The girls will usually show up, call the boys immature and tut at them until they figure out their rankings; once this has been 'sussed', they will then pair up with their opposite number. If there is an odd number of male to female, a left-over male chav generally resorts to abusive name-calling to amuse himself, referring to the female minis as a bunch of 'slappers' or 'scummy bints'. This will continue until he bores of the sport and returns home. A left-over 'female mini, however, will either cry or sit in silence, telling everyone else later that her friends are just a bunch of slags, and that she only ever goes with older men, anyway!

Second, **The Town Centre** – this is where mini chavs establish their base camp – usually a bench that is in close proximity to McDonald's – as early as possible (around 11 a.m.) because turf wars can often be fought over prime Saturday perching spots. Pack leaders will then send out scouting parties to JJB Sports and Game for the boys, or Tammy Girl and Superdrug for the girls. When the shops are closed, to stop themselves going stir crazy, these chavs have to be inventive and find alternative hang-outs like bus or train stations. Here they will encounter ordinary people who want to use these locations in the more traditional way,

Bus and train stations are popular alternative chav hangouts.

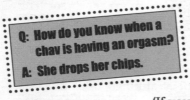

Q: How do you know when a chav is having an orgasm?

A: She drops her chips.

but if they show any sign of fear or are intimidated, the mini-chav gangs can turn nasty. The best defence is to pretend that you are one of them but a bit more scary. (If you suspect that you are going to be in this situation, you should make sure you dress as they do, but don't wear too much designer gear if you want to avoid being mugged.) An alternative form of defence would be to pretend that you are a lunatic and have just escaped from the local asylum. NB: this tactic will only work if you pretend to be a very *dangerous* lunatic. Weak-looking lunatics can provide hours of unadulterated amusement for your average mini-chav gang, which is seriously bad news!

16-45 – The Breeding Years

As we all know, if the female chav doesn't have a child by the time she is seventeen, she will be viewed as an infertile freak by her immediate community. Maternity wards have taken this age issue into account and now provide GCSE textbooks as reading material in their waiting rooms. But given that chav blokes will only accept the stepchildren if they also have one of 'their own', female chavs tend to breed for many years in order to stay in the dating game. This often leads to vast age differences amongst chav siblings. In fact, sometimes there can be as much as twenty years between brothers and sisters and it is not uncommon for chavlings to have

aunts and uncles who are far younger than they are. So, alongside the GCSE textbooks you might also find SAGA holiday brochures.

Traditionally, the female chav will have had her first sprog by the age of seventeen and another will follow at nineteen. They usually say they 'wanna 'ave a fam'ly, innit'. The actual reason for having a second

child is to get full use out of the baby walker and highchair, or to use one of the other baby names they'd picked last time. In a kind of genetic experiment to see if they can make the next kid less horrifically naughty as the first one, or maybe just because the female chavster fancies a bit of a change, this new baby will usually have a different father to the first one. However, on the rare occasion when a male chav sticks around long enough to have a second baby with his chav partner, everyone will consider this union to be one of true love. Their 'Love Conquers All' story invariably ends up being sent to a magazine who has advertised for 'Your True Life' stories and is willing to pay £100 to publish it.

And just as it is in the animal kingdom, there is one strong breeding male per community and all the females will try their very best to have a baby by him. (If they manage to get two babies by him, it is customary for other chav females to come and pay homage to the couple.) In reality, the male chav's usual pattern of breeding is to try to knock up as many females in as small a radius as possible. As all chavs tend to look the same anyway, this doesn't really pose too much of a problem until schooldays arrive for the offspring of these unions. On a first day at school the chavling can find himself in a class with at least three other siblings – although usually the chavling only knows of the existence of one of them as a blood relative. Other than the fun that can be had with gossip about this, the situation doesn't really cause too many problems until the youngsters get to breeding age. Only then,

*

It is not uncommon for chavlings to have aunts and uncles who are far younger than they are.

*

*

The male chav's usual pattern of breeding is to try and knock up as many females in as small a radius as possible.

*

when parents discover the awful truth about who their Jason has been shagging, will they have to own up and insist that the liaison ends. (If they are ashamed of owning up to the potential incest factor, they will try to put their chav son off their new girlfriend because 'Becky-Leah is a tart who everyone knows shagged your mate and your cousin)'.

✱

Chavs will always buy their food supplies from the local corner shop - paying as much as twice the price for some things than they would if they'd made the journey to their local supermarket.

✱

Neither male nor female chav breeders will usually have jobs and will, therefore, have plenty of time to shop. Although they will spend as much time in the town centre as other chavs, they will always buy their food supplies from the local corner shop – paying as much as twice the price for some things than they would if they'd made the journey to their local supermarket. In fact, the only reason chavs seem to go to supermarkets is to annoy everyone else as they scream at their kids and crash about with their trolleys.

The shopping ritual begins quite early in the day (around 11 a.m.). This is when chavs can be spotted visiting the local corner shop and leaving shortly afterwards with an incredibly thin-to-breaking-point white carrier bag containing two bottles of cheap cider and forty fags. This will be enough to see them through until 4 p.m. when the kids are back from school. Chavs show great loyalty to their local shops – not for any altruistic reason, but because these shop owners will often give them credit within hours of cashing in – and spending – their weekly giros.

Chavs in this age range may miss having a place to hang out, and instead of the swing park they will usually choose the Social Security offices or the Job Centre, where little damage can be done as the seats are bolted to the floor. There is no need for sign-posted directions to these places as there will always be at least four or five chavs smoking and looking furtive at the entrance at any

one time. Not showing up at either location for over a week is sufficient enough for the police to list the chav as a missing person.

In order to alleviate the boredom of having little purpose to their daily lives, the female chavster will need to have an enemy. Indeed, if a chav ever takes the time to look at their life and feels that something is missing, they will always conclude that there is someone somewhere to blame and that someone will need to pay for the misery they've caused. Unlike their mini counterparts, chavs in this age range will not always pick on the weakest of the bunch; they want a worthy opponent, someone who will join them in a feud that will, with luck, last for many years. There isn't often an actual starting point to any such 'war', but if pressed, a chav will recall some minor 'funny' comment about their man, their kids, their pets or their house. In desperate circumstances, a funny look will do, and they will replicate this look at each other like two dogs about to fight for years to come. In fact, some of these feuds can last so long and get so many people involved that half the participants have to be moved by the council to the far reaches of the country to prevent the feud from escalating into a full-blown civil war. Of course, if all these arguments were to stop, ITV Chav would be hard pressed to find entertaining subjects to film their fly-on-the-wall documentaries.

45-Death – The Twilight Years

In the same way that you never see baby pigeons, you also never see sweet old chav folk. They just don't seem to exist. Perhaps chavs mellow out to such an extent that they simply stop being chavs. Therefore any reference to the final age of chav simply means those who can't still 'sprog up'.

If you do spot old chavs (you might find one towing a fake-Burberry bag-on-wheels shopper), they're likely to look like a very wrinkly, baggy

*

The words 'mutton' and 'lamb' will jump into the minds of all who see old chavs tottering down the high street in clothes that are more suited to your average twenty-year-old chavster.

*

version of their children. (They're baggy due to excess sagging skin – which can make their tattoos somewhat difficult to read!) And the words 'mutton' and 'lamb' will jump into the minds of all who see them tottering down the high street in clothes that are more suited to your average twenty-year-old chavster.

Alternatively, they will let it all go to hell and take up the old chav uniform of 1980s: shiny shell suit, complete with gold chains that are so heavy they have to lug them about like Marley's ghost.

These old female chavs will profess to love their grandchildren more than anything else in the world and, even more than their daughters, will enjoy starting rows over the little chavlings. Who has the most grandchildren and great-grandchildren, and who had them earliest, are great sources of competition. The winner is the one who can't name all their multitude.

As older people can be quite frail, ageing chavs will often use this fact to their advantage. In fact, having 'fallen over', they will contact the 'no-win-no-fee' claims company as often as possible. In reality, however, the average old chav doesn't seem to suffer too greatly from any form of age-related illness such as dementia. Indeed, the reason behind this sprightly mental state seems to be because someone has to keep watch over who can partner who 'legally', and most make a point of remembering quite clearly all the enemies they have amassed over the years. But as chavs do everything a little bit earlier than most ordinary folk, their life expectancy tends to be fairly short. This could be due to poor health and living conditions, but the more likely cause is that they simply run out of people to argue with.

Chav Quiz Time

It's all very well knowing how to spot chavs in the wild, but what if – by some bizarre coincidence – you've started to suspect that you have chav tendencies – or heaven forbid, that you actually are a chav!? You have two options: stop all chav-type behaviour immediately and purge yourself of baseball caps, bling, scrunchies, etc. Or you can embrace the truth and revel in your newly discovered chav status. Either way, knowledge is power – so if you're in any doubt check out your chav rating with this handy quiz. It will also help to recap on just some of the aspects of chav culture we've observed ...

Recap? Is dat a kinna baseball cap denn?

Question one: You've opened your eyes on a brand new day. What do you see?

1

a) I'm in my bedroom, the air smells fresh and I can see my Ikea wardrobe, replete with freshly laundered clothes. I'm lying next to my spouse and my children are still sleeping peacefully in their beds. When I get up, I quickly prepare a round of toast and some cereal for the kids before they rush off to school.

b) I'm lying on my futon. Next to me will be my non-sex-specific partner who I love and respect. From my window, I can see the peaceful meadows outside and have a longing to rush out and commune with nature. When I get up I will prepare a delicious bowl of organic muesli and wheatgrass juice from the newly sprouted seeds I've grown.

c) I'm lying on the sofa. Next to me is a person with whom I may or may not have exchanged bodily fluids. Around me are some old beer cans, an overflowing ashtray and the remains of last night's curry. As I try to prise my eyelids open, the kids are screaming and I have an urgent need to vomit.

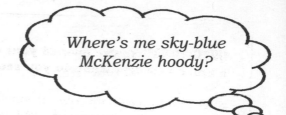

Where's me sky-blue McKenzie hoody?

Question two: After your morning ablutions, you take a peek inside your wardrobe to decide what to wear. But what will you choose?

2

a) Much will depend on the weather and what I'll be doing that day, but generally I'll opt for something from Next or Marks & Spencer – smart/casual and easy to wear.

b) Whatever the weather, I'd choose something from my range of tye-dye kaftans, teamed with a large shaggy Afghan-type cardigan and plastic shoes. (As a supporter of the ethical treatment of animals, I couldn't possibly wear leather!) Anything I choose will be produced in a non-oppressive collective.

c) I'll choose something from the market that has a designer name on it – even if it looks completely fake and tacky – which will match my fake tan and tacky 'bling'.

Question three: You look in the food cupboards and refrigerator and find them lacking. You need to do some shopping. Where do you go to purchase your supplies?

3

a) I'll probably go to one of the major supermarket chains – or a nearby Marks & Spencer food hall – and, in order to save my time and energy, I'll buy enough food to last me through the week.

b) Everything I eat has to be as fresh as possible, and organic, of course, so I'll buy just enough food to last me for one day. I'll opt to buy from a farmers' market or from somewhere that I know small traders can make a fair profit.

c) If I can be arsed, I might get a pasty or a pie from the local shop, but if pushed, will descend upon the local supermarket to stock up on some economy beans, burgers and oven chips. Realistically, I'll probably end up daahn the kebab shop or the chippie.

Am gaaahna MaccyD's for a chazz burgaa!

What's me Chesney dooin' on page three?

Question four: As you don't have anything planned for the day, you decide it might be nice to relax with a coffee and a newspaper. But which one?

4

a) Despite raising my blood pressure, I'll choose the *Mail*, because I can rely on it to keep me posted on the issues of the day, like money-grabbing asylum seekers and how much I can expect to pay for little Tamzin's school fees next year.

b) The *Guardian*, because I can rely on it to expose all the underhand tricks being played on the poor unsuspecting public by the government – and it encourages me to have a bit of a rant!

c) The *Sun*, because it has loads of well nice pictures (great big knockers and sneaky paparazzi stuff), which saves me the trouble of reading any of the articles to see what's going on in the world of celebrity, sport and gossip. And I get a sneak preview of what's gonna 'appen next in *'Stenders*.

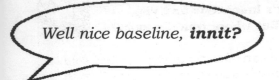

*Well nice baseline, **innit?***

Question five: It's mid-morning and the phone rings. You're expecting to hear from...

5

a) My sister. She's probably discovered a great new patisserie that's just opened nearby, and wants to suggest we meet there of our mid-morning lattes.

b) My crystal healer. She's likely to have received a message from the cosmos again, which indicates that my aura is definitely out of sync and advises that I spend a few hours meditating under my Big Blue Aura Triangle.

c) My kids' school. They are probably demanding that I dash over to prise little TasHar's teeth from the teacher's ankle again.

Question six: It's lunchtime and you fancy a treat. But where would you go?

6

a) Anywhere that can offer me the type of food sold in Marks & Spencer – and where I can treat myself to a nice cream cake and then tell everyone how naughty I am for eating it!

b) A vegan wholefood café that serves nutritious, delicious green-looking food – and where I can meet the rest of my pressure group there and plan my letter writing campaigns.

c) Maccy D's where I will make a Happy Meal last two hours so that me and my blinged-up mate can bitch about all the other customers.

Question seven: Back home, you put some music on. What are you listening to?

7

a) Norah Jones, or perhaps some cool jazz sounds.

b) Some folksy music from Peru, or create 'energy' sounds of my own with my bongos, panpipes and tambourine.

c) Some banging 'choons'. Doesn't really matter what, but the baseline must be pounding and loud enough to crack the house foundations.

Question eight: Perhaps you'd prefer to watch some television? But what's on?

a) Anything that's currently popular and making the headlines – but nothing too tacky. It's always good to be able to start dinner party conversations with 'Oooh, did you see...?'

b) Anything environmentally friendly and politically correct. Generally, non-sexist, non-racist, non-homophobic.

c) Anything on ITV or Sky One. Preferably something 'From Hell' (Pets, Neighbours, Hairdressers, etc). Something involving wife swapping is also a must-see!

Question nine: A night out at the cinema is an appealing prospect. What would you choose to see?

a) Something light, fun and British – like *Calendar Girls* or *Four Weddings and a Funeral*.

b) Anything with subtitles that has a running time of over four hours and which is breaking new boundaries with experimental photography and soundtracks.

c) Anything that's a sequel and has masses of violence, blood, crashing cars, sawn-off shotguns and kung fu fighting.

10

Question ten: It's time for bed, but what's the routine?

a) Teeth brushed, PJs on and a nice bit of light reading before lights out at 11 p.m.

b) A little transcendental meditation, a cup of herbal tea and then a gentle chant under my 100% cotton fibre duvet before sleep claims me.

c) Furious rows, music banging out, or best of all, encouraging the dog to bark until 2 a.m. This is when you start to doze off in front of a Jean-Claude Van Damme video with yesterday's make-up smeared around your chops.

Soon be time for Trisha

ANSWERS

If you've answered...

Mostly As – You wouldn't enter Argos if your life depended on it and are actively proud that the chavs would refer to you as a 'blaahddy stuck-up old caa'. You're a middle-class muddler with no chav tendencies.

Mostly Bs – You are the worthy hippy-dippy type and are probably referred to as 'a bit of a nuisance' by most people. Since you wouldn't go near a value burger and are prepared to pay a bit extra for clothes not produced in third world sweatshops, you can't be a chav. But beware! Chavs can spot an easy target, so don't let your respect for all humanity lure you into a chav-type 'soft-touch' trap!

Mostly Cs – You are of course a chav and proud to be one! Chances are you only bought this book to see if it could help you rise in chav ranks. Or else you got a 'five finger discount'! (i.e. – you nicked it!)

About the Authors

Mia and Clint met three years ago in a branch of McDonald's where they set themselves apart from the usual clientele by ordering burgers that cost more than a 'paaand'. Deciding they were kindred spirits cast adrift in a sea of scrunchies, baseball caps and bling, they began a quest to seek out chavish behaviour and laugh at it wherever possible. This led to the creation of the chav website – chavscum.co.uk – in December 2003. This site has proved to be extremely popular and is the internet's premiere site for pics of chavs in the wild.

In a recent mission statement Mia likened herself to Sigourney Weaver in the film *Gorillas in the Mist*, because she tries to integrate herself in the chav community and gain their trust in order to observe their behaviour. Strangely, Clint also likens himself to Sigourney Weaver. However, he connects more with her role in the film *Alien* as he tries to locate the queen chav's nest so that he can get rid of her eggs and call her a bitch.